DECONSTRUCTING
RELIGION

Derrick Day

Deconstructing Religion
by
Derrick Day

Published by Kingdom Covenant International

All Scripture cited in this work is taken from the King James Bible unless otherwise noted.

All instances of the name "satan" are deliberately not capitalized.

Other Books by the Author:

satan, Let Me Refresh Your Memory (with Angela Day)
Turn into the Skid (2017)
Grace Discipleship (2017)

CONTENTS

FOREWORD

D ear reader,

A few years ago, I had some work done in my backyard. The gentleman who was over the project had sketched out a plan of how everything would look. On paper, it was beautiful. A few days later, the crew showed up and within one hour, my yard was a mess! I walked outside and probably had a puzzled look on my face. The landscaper came up to me and said something that is profound: "Terry, before we can CONSTRUCT, we must first DESTRUCT." Sure enough, it all worked out beautifully.

That is exactly what Derrick Day has done in this book. Before you can CONSTRUCT the proper image of God, you must first DESTRUCT the image religion has formed. It may look messy at first. Just wait! It all works out beautifully.

One of my biggest "pet peeves" is hearing people accuse God for things that would get any earthly father locked up in prison for doing. I have often said that I'll pay anyone $10,000.00 if they can show me anywhere in the four gospels (Matthew, Mark, Luke and John) where Jesus, who is THE true expression of God, EVER put sickness, disease, depression, storms or poverty on anyone to "teach" them, "perfect" them or to bring about a greater good. Guess what? I still have my $10,000.00. No one has ever been able to show me. Yet, millions are indoctrinated by a religious system that tells them "God is your problem."

That is why I strongly support Derrick Day's book, Deconstructing Religion. How do you describe a book that tackles major questions in which "holy wars" have been fought and he so eloquently gives answers that a 1st grader could understand? Only one word will do: Masterpiece! This book is a-w-e-s-o-m-e! I could write my own book explaining how much I love this book.

To summarize: If you are looking to go, not to the next level, but to the ultimate level of faith, hope and love, THIS IS A MUST READ! It's been said that a picture is worth a thousand words. One of Derrick Day's words in this book paints a thousand pictures of God's love, grace and abounding life He has made available for us to experience in Christ. Not only is there depth in his writing, Derrick gives the practical know how in order to live in the reality you were created for. Not a set of rules, but a living relationship with a loving Father.

If you have ever asked questions like:

Why did God give The Law? What's the Tithe thing all about? What is "Strange Fire"? If God controls EVERYTHING then why are things so crazy? Why is there a hell? Who is it for? What is true repentance? What is holiness? Are we to sit and wait for the Lord's return or are we to takeover with His authority? What about women preachers? GET THIS BOOK! It is filled with wisdom and understanding that will enrich your life, and the lives of others you influence.

Terry Tripp
Terry Trip Ministries
www.terrytripp.com

DEDICATION

This book has truly been a labor of love! During its writing, My Wife, Angela – who is also my Best Friend, my Lover, and my Partner in Ministry – suffered with my late nights and fits of impatience. She is my biggest cheerleader and my toughest critic. This book would never have been finished without her.

I'm also grateful for and to my sons, Donovan, Zachary, Derrick II, Anthony, and Troy. I am blessed to know that the things God has shared with me have made a lasting impact in their lives.

To my Mother, Shirley Day, thanks for bringing me into this world and for your love and determination. My love for reading and writing began with you.

I'm grateful to my Dad, Richard Day, and my Mom, Odessa Day, for never allowing me to settle for mediocrity.

To my siblings, Sandra, Morris, Jesse, Bryan, Michelle, Darryl, and Dewayne. Y'all are the best! I love you all.

I also want to thank the Agape Dominion Family. They have consistently cheered me on and have provided a sounding board for most of the material in this book. I am blessed to pastor the World's Greatest Church.

To my mentors, Ed Delph, Robert Ricciardelli, and Terry Tripp, thanks for giving me advice and education that money can't buy.

To my "inner circle," Patrick Joubert, Marshall Stukes III, Jeremiah Johnson, David Singer, Bill Thomas, Troy Anthony Smith, Ulysses "Jack" Howard, Eric Schlebus, Carlos Howard, Frank Nelson, Paul Wilson, Matthew Moore, Jr., Robert Upton, Paul Freeman, George Waddles Jr., Joshua Maynard, Anthony Calloway, Royce Robinson, Sabaran Steger, Matthew Ray, Richardo Griffith, Fred Willis, Thomas Anthony Burns, Tony Newton, Tom Tompkins, Laymon Hornsby, Keith Williams, Mark Hicks, Darryl Rivers, James Johnson, Jay Ross, Wayne Daniels, Jr., Jay Guy, Henry Harris, "Nor'West Prophetic" and "Praying Medic," thanks for your counsel, encouragement, and edification.

I'm grateful for some great preachers who have impacted my life, Reverend Samuel Washington, Sr., Bo Thompson, Bishop Napoleon Rhodes, Dr. Billy L. Bell, Dr. Bernie Wade, Don Nori, Sr, Dr. Barney Phillips, Dr. Roy Smith, Phil Munsey, Bishop Craig Soaries, Dr. DeForest Sories, James Hutchins, Ben Tankard, Bishop Daniel Ubon-Abasi, and Dr. Ralph Day.

Thanks to my other "Mothers," Florence Ruffin, Claudine Smith, and the late Gloria Rushing and Marilynn Sims for loving me as if I were their own son.

To my In-Laws, Jerry and Vivian Woolbright, I'm grateful for trusting me with your daughter's hand.

To Anthony and Mary – I'm blessed to call you Brother and Sister.

To my Uncles, Arthur, Steven, Abron, Bill, Eddie, Rodney, Willie, Clifton, David, Otis, Frank, and Detroit, thanks for your wise counsel.

To my Aunts, Yvonne, Danya, Heidi, Andrea, Gwen, Rose, Sylvia, Marie, Regina, Maggie, Ruby, Darlene, Deni, Marcia, Sharon, Tami, Lisa, Denise, Shirley, Patricia, Albertine, Effie, and "Petey," I love and cherish you all.

Thanks, Bernard Rushing, Sr. (Pops) for showing me what being a husband and father is.

To Leon, Inman, Dalton, Bernard Jr., Charles, Malinda, William, Kevin, Renee, Toney, Henry, and Danny. Y'all are thicker than blood!

To Gloria, Jackie, and Ty – marriage made us family but Love keeps us that way!

Thanks to Brenda Andrews and Leonard Colvin of the New Journal and Guide, and to Tony Macrini and Bob Sinclair of WNIS-790 for giving me the opportunity to write and speak to broad audiences. I'm also grateful to Barbara Hamm, Barbara Ciara, Kurt Williams, Joel Rubin, and Karen Quiñones-Miller for their support in all things journalistic.

Thanks to Erick Terry, Brad Garrison, Adam Derositte, Josh Bowerman, Kenneth Johnson, Jeff Hastings, and "Kenpo" Ken Thomas for their warrior training and input.

To Tiffany and Tameka, I'm blessed that we're reconnected.

To all my cousins, nieces, and nephews – I love you all!

To the late Bertha Washington, Martha Stoudemire, Arthur Day, Sr., Gloria Day, Robert Ross Stoudemire, Sr., Lauretta "Mickey" Day, Elnora Stoudemire, Drayton D. Stoudemire, I, Lauretta Verdier, Clifford Verdier, Daniel Ruffin, III, Florence "Georgia" Ruffin, Robert Ed Stoudemire, Grant Toyer, Sr., Ramona Stoudemire, Gloria Jean Adams, Horace Livingston, Jr. and Drayton D. Stoudemire, II, I hope y'all are proud of me.

Thanks to Freeze, Tori, Monte, and Jellybean, for the love and the music.

I also want to give a shoutout to Tony Brown of "Tony Brown's Journal," who once gave a word of encouragement to me when I was a young, zealous activist.

Most of all, I'm grateful to my Heavenly Father, my Big Brother and Savior, Jesus, and the Holy Spirit.

I pray you're just as blessed in reading it as I was in writing it!

– Bishop Derrick Day

INTRODUCTION

The Church is at a pivotal moment in its history. Once the pinnacle of society, the Church is now almost an historical footnote. How did this happen? It happened because the Church embraced doctrine that minimized the command of Jesus to go into the world and demonstrate the Kingdom of God with power and authority. It happened because the Church embraced religion over Kingdom relationship.

The Church has effectively become the bastion of the legalistic religion that Jesus came to displace.

The Body of Christ has moved farther and farther away from what Jesus, Paul, or any of the Apostles taught, supplanting the doctrine of Jesus with traditions of men. And, just as Jesus warned, these traditions have nullified the power of the Word of God.

The purpose of the church was to be the seat of God's government in the earth. In a physical sense, it should be a hospital for the spiritually sick, a place of resurrection for the spiritually dead, and a refuge for the saints. Instead it has become a country club for the religious and a museum for the "frozen chosen."

Jesus is called "The Chief Cornerstone" but, over time, folks have taken this cornerstone and painted it as they've seen fit. After the first-century Church, someone came along with a doctrine that painted the cornerstone a new color; most everyone agreed this coloring was good. But this process was repeated over and over, throughout centuries, until the cornerstone is no longer recognizable due to the veneers applied to Christ.

Added to the distortion of the cornerstone of our faith has been added doctrine and dogma, much of which has been built around situational text. One thing I've discovered is when you take a scripture out of context and build doctrine around it, you move from proper exegesis (critical explanation or interpretation of a text) of Scripture to eisegesis (the process of interpreting a text such that it introduces agendas and biases). This, ultimately, leads to the building of a religious construct.

This distortion of Christ has led to widespread powerlessness and irrelevance. The Church is no longer the destination for the destitute or the haven for the hurting. The Church has – by and large – abandoned teaching of healing and reconciliation, and is no longer is the liberator of captives of sin and the law. Instead, the Church has become a stern taskmaster who tries to take souls from slavery to sin to servants of religion.

This gross misinterpretation of the person of Jesus Christ must be completely obliterated. Jesus, Himself, is the foundation for our faith but the church has been remade in the image of men. Often times, a building framed out of plumb and out of level can be successfully renovated; other times, it must be deconstructed down to its foundation and rebuilt.

The premise of this book is the Church has reached a point that it is so rife with religion that it must be disassembled to its foundation – Jesus Christ – and rebuilt according to the first-century blueprint. Religion must be deconstructed to restore the revelation of the Gospel.

This book aims to strip away the veneer that has clouded and obscured – and, ultimately, deconstruct the incorrect doctrine built around – the one person who can change the world and restore the Church to its place of prominence: JESUS!

Religion and the Church

Matthew 16:18
And I say also unto thee, That thou art Peter, and upon this rock I will build my church; and the gates of hell shall not prevail against it.

WHAT IS CHURCH?

Ask many people what do they do on Sunday morning and they will tell you they go to church. And, if you ask them why do they go to church, you'll get a variety of answers: "To worship." "To fellowship." "To hear from God."

All of these are good answers but, guess what; you can do these things anywhere. Why?

Let me tell you!

> *13 Now when Jesus came into the district of Caesarea Philippi, he asked his disciples, "Who do people say that the Son of Man*

13

is?" 14 And they said, "Some say John the Baptist, others say Elijah, and others Jeremiah or one of the prophets." 15 He said to them, "But who do you say that I am?" 16 Simon Peter replied, "You are the Christ, the Son of the living God." 17 And Jesus answered him, "Blessed are you, Simon Bar-Jonah! For flesh and blood has not revealed this to you, but my Father who is in heaven. 18 And I tell you, you are Peter, and on this rock I will build my church, and the gates of hell shall not prevail against it. 19 I will give you the keys of the kingdom of heaven, and whatever you bind on earth shall be bound in heaven, and whatever you loose on earth shall be loosed in heaven." (Matthew 16:13-20 ESV)

Here, we will see that the Church is God's Government on earth, it is the Bride of Christ, and it is His Children. And that it isn't restricted to buildings.

Government

In verse 18 of this chapter's text, Jesus is saying that upon this rock, He will build His church.

Quick stop here: this and verse 19 are where we get the concept of St. Peter manning the gate to Heaven. Unfortunately for many, this just isn't true. What Jesus is saying to Peter is that he is a rock but upon a bigger rock (the truth, that is, Jesus, Himself); that He will build His Church. There is no solid scriptural evidence that the church would be built upon Peter.

14

Moving right along – the Greek word for Church is *ekklesia*. This word literally means "called out assembly." The Roman Empire called its legislative body by this term. Jesus isn't speaking of something religious, here; He's speaking of a new Government. This is why He preached so much about the Kingdom of God being at hand – or here-and-now.

This harmonizes with what Jesus commanded:

> *And he said to them, "Go into all the world and proclaim the gospel to the whole creation. (Mark 16:15 ESV)*

The imperative, here, is GO. Jesus did not restore a seated Kingdom on earth; He brought forth a mobile one. Notice Jesus' example: He went from place to place, preaching and teaching. He did not have a set "base of operations."

Jesus did not say, "If you build it, they will come…" That ain't the Gospel, that's "Field of Dreams!"

The Government of God is focused on taking Jesus to people not getting people to come to church!

Bride

The Church is the Bride of Christ. She is to be presented to Him without spot or wrinkle (Ephesians 5:27).

It is incumbent upon the bride to prepare (Revelation 19:7). When my Wife and I got married, I didn't have to participate in her preparation. That was her responsibility. My responsibility was to make a place for her and provide for her. We, the church are responsible for preparing ourselves for the wedding!

We are to be married to Him, to Love Him, and be faithful to Him. Not out of fear of reprisal:

> *There is no fear in love, but perfect love casts out fear. For fear has to do with punishment, and whoever fears has not been perfected in love. (1 John 4:18 ESV)*

You cannot be prepared to spend eternity with someone you fear!

Children

Romans 8:14 tells us that if the Spirit leads us, we are sons of God. We are to reflect his will, culture, and intent in the world.

Those who are born again have the very DNA of God in them (Romans 8:21). God loves us so much that it wasn't enough for him to position Himself close to us; He chose, instead, to place Himself within us.

As a father, I can tell you that my sons looking like me is a blessing but where I'm really blessed is when they reflect my influence. We are all created in the image of God (to look like Him) but He is really glorified when we manifest the fruit of His Spirit (acting like Him – Galatians 5:22-23).

Every parent wishes for their influence to be greater than the world's in the life of their children God is no different. Romans 8:19 tells us that all creation groans for the manifestation of the sons of God. In other words, all of God's creation is waiting for His kids to show up and take authority!

We are the church!

What Church is Not

Paul teaches in 1 Corinthians 6:19 that our bodies are the temple of the Holy Spirit. Hebrews 10:10 says we are sanctified once for all by Jesus' perfect offering. Nowhere in the New Covenant is there spoken of a consecrated (set apart) building. Acts 7:48 tells us that God does not dwell in houses made by hands of men. No, God dwells in the hearts of men, made by the Hands of God!

Simply put, Church is not a building!

Don't get me wrong, buildings are fine. But a church building is no more sanctified than a person's home, a courtroom, or a shopping center. But if there are more believers in a Walmart than there are in a church building, which is more sanctified?

We need to be careful that we do not get into building– or people-worship. Better yet, we shouldn't succumb to the mindset of worshiping worship.

Jesus said – before the cross – that where two or more are gathered in His name, there He is in the midst. However, after the cross, the Holy Spirit dwells in every believer! So, Jesus goes wherever we are! And wherever we stand is holy ground because we sanctify it with the Spirit of God dwelling in us.

But the church is not a building led by a man, it is an organic body led by Christ. Buildings are made of dead material; the Body of Christ is made up of living souls. The Church is not a place of worship; it is the body of saints who worship!

Pastor Tony Evans said it best; church is like the huddle in football. It is where God calls the play and sends it in through His quarterback, the preacher or pastor. Once we get the play, we go out into the world and run the play – then we come back the following Sunday and debrief on how successful we were.

That said, the church is, perhaps, the most misunderstood institution on earth.

THE MISUNDERSTOOD INSTITUTION

T he Church remains one of the most easily recognized and influential organizations in many communities. It is also, perhaps, the most misunderstood.

The Church was the source of social welfare assistance before that baton was unceremoniously passed on to government. It was considered the paragon of social virtue.

The reason why many "churches" do not have the nature of The Church is because there is a widespread lack of

19

understanding of what The Church really is. Like its members, the Church suffers from an identity crisis that has resulted in an "orphan mentality;" lacking knowledge of its true parentage and associated privilege.

First of all, The Church is not a building, a charter, or a gathering of folks. The Church is a living, spiritual and natural being comprised of many members that carry out vital functions.

Contrary to popular belief and contemporary manifestation, The Church is not the "sanctuary" for the "pseudo-sanctified." When you become a member of The Church, you are not simply a number; you are grafted in, as a finger to a hand. You are part of a glorious body. This body nourishes each member and the Head, Jesus, gives each member instructions for the work to be performed.

While I'm here, let me hang my hat for a minute...Each member has a UNIQUE function. All of us are not called to preach, just like every cell in the body is not called to be the eye. Imagine a body full of eyes...that is a freak of nature! Speaking of the ministry, not everyone is called to preach the same message or even to preach in the same manner. Each of us is fearfully and wonderfully designed – individually and expressly – by the Hand of God with a unique purpose to carry out equally unique assignments.

Jesus did not come to establish another religion; the world had (and has) enough of them. What He came to re-establish was the governmental order that was ordained from the foundation of time!

20

That said, The Church is not about religion. The Church is the point where God connects with man through Christ. It is God's earthly government, duly deputized and empowered to have dominion over the earth!

Church should be an emergency room for the wounded, a kitchen for the hungry, and a sanctuary for the besieged. It should be the point where God's Heavenly Government is dispensed on the earth. It should be the place where the lost can come to catch the revelation of a loving Father, who wants to reconcile them to Himself and loved them so much that He gave His very best in the Person of His Only Begotten Son!

There are many who focus on the history and the traditions of the church. While it's good to understand history in order to determine direction, dwelling on history causes stagnation.

THE RELIGION OF CHURCH HISTORY

C hurch history is good information, albeit as a sidebar. The more pressing issues are how to effectively reach the lost and holistically minister to the saints. To use a natural example to illustrate a spiritual truth: the surgeon, while well versed in medical history, does not have the luxury of historical retrospection when the patient is on the operating table.

Historical perspective is essential in preparation and a luxury in debriefing, but almost useless in the theatre of battle. I think two of the biggest issues facing the modern church are a tendency to contemplate history and an inflation of ecumenical protocol. I understand the point of historical study on the part of some but I think that it is overwrought by many others.

My issue is not with history, rather the application of it. History is important, to be sure, but I have concerns about so many men and women of God bogged down in history and ecumenical affairs to the point that it draws our attention from more needful matters.

When you look out and see that folks are dying – literally – from homicide, AIDS, cancer, suicide, traffic accidents and so forth, how is dedicated discussion of church history pertinent to that? Folks are dying without Jesus! We need sound preaching and teaching, not history lessons.

If we get mired in historical discussions, we will invariably head down the denomination path, and God only knows where that rabbit hole will lead.

No, we need to be ministering the Gospel of the Kingdom and the full counsel of God to this sick and dying world. We need to be about what Jesus said do – healing the sick, cleansing lepers, raising the dead, and preaching the Gospel to the Poor. While we sit up in our ivory towers of learning discussing history, the world is dying without any understanding of Jesus and His salvation.

No discussion on church fathers and church history is going to get anyone saved, healed, delivered or prospered. Again, not saying historical discussion is not meaningful, just that there are more important things to do.

23

While we're discussing history and tradition, we would do well to understand the religious jargon and rhetoric that permeates the church.

RELIGIOUS RHETORIC

The contemporary church is terribly lacking in dialogue. God said to Isaiah, "come let us reason together" (Isaiah 1:18). If God calls us to reason with Him, why, then, don't we talk to each other? There are some serious issues that are facing this sick and dying world and "church as usual" isn't helping!

We have Christ-averse religions growing and seeking to expand their reach into the fabric of our nation and we simply say, "Can we all just get along?" Yes, we can but we must preach the Gospel! Jesus drew the line in the sand in John 14:6, when He said "I am the way, the truth, and the life: no man cometh unto the Father but by me."

Christianity is not just another religion; it is a way of life. Better yet, it is THE WAY TO LIFE! We must be loving and civil but we must preach the truth nonetheless. Instead of allowing religion to make inroads into our communities, we need to push back gently, explaining that Jesus is not a way, He is THE WAY!

We have young men killing each other at an alarming rate. More and more young people are incarcerated and, thus, indoctrinated into a life of recidivism. Black women have the highest rate of HIV-AIDS in the country. Depression runs rampant. Suicide is on the rise. All the while we wring our collective hands, quoting scripture and doing nothing. There should be living examples of how the church is mentoring young people into leadership, counseling of our youth on how to maintain sexual purity, and how the joy of the Lord can break the strongholds of depression and suicide. These are the things that require our immediate attention and resources.

Religious rhetoric will no longer cut it. The full Gospel of the Kingdom of God must be preached; that Gospel is the Gospel of wholeness and completion in the earth; not lack today and deferred reward in the "sweet-by-and-by." THE GOSPEL is the message of God's unconditional Love and Grace. It is only the understanding that God loves us completely and has extended His unmerited favor toward us that will change the world.

Change requires action. We can no longer afford to stand on the sidelines and hope that either things will simply change themselves or government will somehow stop the societal train-wreck. Change will not be instantaneous;

initially the impact of the Kingdom will be incremental and unseen. However, if we are faithful about prosecuting the Kingdom agenda, incremental changes will swell into significant, visible changes that will impact and influence the world.

Imagine if – instead of picketing abortion clinics, calling the women "sluts" and "whores" – we setup quiet places nearby where we could minister the love of God to women contemplating abortion. Imagine if we were to tell them how much God loves them and so do we. Imagine if we told them that God has an awesome plan for both mother and baby. Imagine if we told them that even if they choose to end their pregnancy, God loves them and so do we. Imagine the hearts and minds such action would change!

Before the church can take action, it must change its consciousness. For centuries, religion has made legions of sin-conscious saints by mixing the covenants of law and Grace. Changing the church requires changing consciousness – from sin-consciousness to righteousness-consciousness. Religion has one major tool in its arsenal to strengthen awareness of sin: The Mosaic law.

LAW AND THE CHURCH

I n this chapter, I will take on a subject that is near and dear to religious traditionalists and flagellants:

The Law of Moses, commonly referred to as "The Law."

The law has a specific use in the New Covenant Church but it is neither a tool for discipleship nor is it a guide for "holy living."

The difference between the Old Covenant and the New Covenant is very similar to the relationship between the Magna Carta (or even the Articles of Confederation) and the U.S. Constitution. The former outlines prophetic precedents and principles that have historical significance (i.e., what you've been delivered from), and the latter outlines the current governing principles.

The Law, when used lawfully (e.g., to show the desperate need for a Savior) is good – even though it has no ability to make anyone righteous or to impart holiness to anyone. However, it is frequently used unlawfully (i.e., as a tool of discipleship). The New Covenant is the revelation of Grace (God's unmerited favor and His unlimited power) and Truth in the person of Jesus Christ. Since all Scripture points to the centrality of the person of Jesus Christ, all Scripture must effectively reveal Him. In other words, the Old Testament is the New Testament concealed and the New Testament is the Old Testament revealed! Jesus is the fulfillment of the Law!

> *But we know that the law is good, if a man use it lawfully; Knowing this, that the law is not made for a righteous man, but for the lawless and disobedient, for the ungodly and for sinners, for unholy and profane, for murderers of fathers and murderers of mothers, for manslayers, For whoremongers, for them that defile themselves with mankind, for menstealers, for liars, for perjured persons, and if there be any other thing that is contrary to sound doctrine; According to the glorious gospel of the blessed God, which was committed to my trust (1 Timothy 1:8-11)*

Legalists will always surface to proclaim the primacy of the law. They incorrectly believe that Saints are saved by

Grace but must be disciple by Law. The Apostles, in the establishment of the first-century Church had to correct this interpretation. Sadly, many Saints experience this same spiritual schizophrenia, today!

> *But there rose up certain of the sect of the Pharisees which believed, saying, That it was needful to circumcise them, and to command them to keep the law of Moses. (Acts 15:5)*

The Law is good and holy. However, it was evidence of God's enmity with man and, as such, it was a curse to man.

> *For as many as are of the works of the law are under the curse: for it is written, Cursed is every one that continueth not in all things which are written in the book of the law to do them. But that no man is justified by the law in the sight of God, it is evident: for, The just shall live by faith. And the law is not of faith: but, The man that doeth them shall live in them. Christ hath redeemed us from the curse of the law, being made a curse for us: for it is written, Cursed is every one that hangeth on a tree: That the blessing of Abraham might come on the Gentiles through Jesus Christ; that we might receive the promise of the Spirit through faith (Galatians 3:10-14)*

No one who has been delivered from a curse should willingly return to it. Yet, that's what the legalist seeks to do when using the Law as a discipleship tool.

> *Having abolished in his flesh the enmity, even the law of commandments contained in ordinances; for to make in himself of twain one new man, so making peace; And that he might reconcile both unto God in one body by the cross, having slain the enmity thereby (Ephesians 2:15-16)*

The purpose of the Law was intended to reveal sin and sin is the source of death.

> *The sting of death is sin; and the strength of sin is the law. (1 Corinthians 15:56)*

Do you see this? The law gives sin a shot of steroids!

Grace, on the other hand, reveals righteousness and is the source of eternal, abundant life!

> *For if by one man's offence death reigned by one; much more they which receive abundance of grace and of the gift of righteousness shall reign in life by one, Jesus Christ. (Romans 5:17)*

The Law is not a ministry of life but of death. And, even though it was holy and glorious, because it did not minister life to the Saints, God abolished it in the lives of His Saints through the ministry of life, the Blood of Jesus!

> *But if the ministration of death, written and engraven in stones, was glorious, so that the children of Israel could not stedfastly behold the face of Moses for the glory of his countenance; which glory was to be done away: How shall not the ministration of the spirit be rather glorious? For if the ministration of condemnation be glory, much more doth the ministration of righteousness exceed in glory. For even that which was made glorious had no glory in this respect, by reason of the glory that excelleth. For if that which is done away was glorious, much more that which remaineth is glorious (2 Corinthians 3:7-11)*

Scripture is clear that the Law was incapable of producing spiritual perfection. If it were, the sacrifice of Jesus would be unnecessary. Indeed, falling back to the law frustrates (renders impotent in that person's life) the Grace of God!

> *I do not frustrate the grace of God: for if righteousness come by the law, then Christ is dead in vain. (Galatians 2:21)*

The Law and its ordinances – and the priesthood responsible for administering it – is flawed because it is dependent upon men and their actions and sacrifices. But Jesus offered a perfect sacrifice that is eternally acceptable for the complete remission of sin and the complete redemption of man. God, through Jesus, took on the entire responsibility of redemption, removing man from the equation!

> *If therefore perfection were by the Levitical priesthood, (for under it the people received the law,) what further need was there that another priest should rise after the order of Melchisedec, and not be called after the order of Aaron? For the priesthood being changed, there is made of necessity a change also of the law (Hebrews 7:11-12)*

> *For the law having a shadow of good things to come, and not the very image of the things, can never with those sacrifices which they offered year by year continually make the comers thereunto perfect (Hebrews 10:1)*

Even Paul was accused of teaching contrary to the Law – because He was! Paul was teaching that the works of the law would never lead to righteousness. It's funny that the Apostle Paul, himself, was persecuted for the same thing that people who teach Grace today, are!

> *And when Gallio was the deputy of Achaia, the Jews made insurrection with one accord against Paul, and brought him to the judgment seat, Saying, This fellow persuadeth men to worship God contrary to the law (Acts 18:12-13)*

> *But now the righteousness of God without*
> *the law is manifested, being witnessed by the*
> *law and the prophets; Even the*
> *righteousness of God which is by faith of*
> *Jesus Christ unto all and upon all them that*
> *believe: for there is no difference (Romans*
> *3:21-22)*

One of the problems resulting from pointing New Covenant Saints to the Old Covenant is that it usually results in works-based, legalistic, religion instead of the liberty that should be revealed in Jesus. This is the mentality Paul was contesting in his letter to the Church at Galatia. Somehow, Judaizing principles (that came from such luminaries as the Apostle Peter, himself) – such as the need for circumcision – crept in and were minimizing the finished work of Jesus.

> *I marvel that ye are so soon removed from*
> *him that called you into the grace of Christ*
> *unto another gospel: Which is not another;*
> *but there be some that trouble you, and*
> *would pervert the gospel of Christ*
> *(Galatians 1:6-7)*

Here, Paul was saying that he marveled – or was amazed – at the fact that the Church at Galatia was even contemplating following the Law after Grace had been introduced and taught to them. It amazes me, too, how anyone can return to Law after tasting Grace.

34

It is Grace through Faith that saves sanctifies, and justifies the Saint, not the Law. Grace and Truth not only came by Jesus Christ but Jesus is, Himself, Grace and Truth!

> *Be it known unto you therefore, men and brethren, that through this man is preached unto you the forgiveness of sins: And by him all that believe are justified from all things, from which ye could not be justified by the law of Moses (Acts 13:38-39).*

> *Knowing that a man is not justified by the works of the law, but by the faith of Jesus Christ, even we have believed in Jesus Christ, that we might be justified by the faith of Christ, and not by the works of the law: for by the works of the law shall no flesh be justified. (Galatians 2:16)*

> *For the law was given by Moses, but grace and truth came by Jesus Christ. (John 1:17)*

Just as when a person emigrating from a foreign land becomes a citizen of a new country, the new birth changes our citizenship from the principality of darkness to the Kingdom of God. And, as such, is subject to an entirely new government. The Kingdom of God is a nation subject to the Grace of the King and not legal ordinances.

> *For sin shall not have dominion over you: for ye are not under the law, but under grace. What then? shall we sin, because we*

are not under the law, but under grace? God
forbid (Romans 6:14-15)

If you're led by flesh (unregenerate), then you are subject to the law. But if you're born-again, you become a Spirit-filled, Spirit-led Kingdom citizen.

But if ye be led of the Spirit, ye are not
under the law. (Galatians 5:18)

And because we who are the Saints of God through Christ have died with Jesus and were raised with Him in the new birth, we have died not only to sin but the Law that exposed them! In the act of being born-again, you die with Christ and are resurrected with Him. As such, you die to the Law and are resurrected into Grace. Contrary to some teaching, you are not a "dead man," you are quickened with Jesus!

Wherefore, my brethren, ye also are become
dead to the law by the body of Christ; that
ye should be married to another, even to him
who is raised from the dead, that we should
bring forth fruit unto God. For when we
were in the flesh, the motions of sins, which
were by the law, did work in our members to
bring forth fruit unto death. But now we are
delivered from the law, that being dead
wherein we were held; that we should serve
in newness of spirit, and not in the oldness
of the letter (Romans 7:4-6)

Indeed, faith is the establishment (foundation), as love is the fulfillment (satisfaction) of the Law. And, since God is Love and Jesus is God in flesh, Jesus, Himself becomes the Law for us, because we abide in Him! And, as the Finished Work of Jesus (Grace) satisfies the debt of sin, it also cancels out the ordinance of the debt, which is the Law. The Finished Work of Jesus was borne by love and, therefore, love is the fulfillment of the Law.

> *Do we then make void the law through faith? God forbid: yea, we establish the law. (Romans 3:31)*

> *Owe no man any thing, but to love one another: for he that loveth another hath fulfilled the law. (Romans 13:8)*

> *Love worketh no ill to his neighbour: therefore love is the fulfilling of the law. (Romans 13:10)*

It is very important for the Saint to understand – that the inheritance promised to us is not by Law but by Promise, and that promise by Faith, and that Faith by Grace. And Faith works by love.

> *For the promise, that he should be the heir of the world, was not to Abraham, or to his seed, through the law, but through the righteousness of faith. For if they which are of the law be heirs, faith is made void, and the promise made of none effect: Because the law worketh wrath: for where no law is,*

there is no transgression. Therefore it is of faith, that it might be by grace; to the end the promise might be sure to all the seed; not to that only which is of the law, but to that also which is of the faith of Abraham; who is the father of us all (Romans 4:13-16)

It is also important to see the things of God cannot be discerned by human flesh, and the Spirit of God – likewise – cannot be received by the Law.

This only would I learn of you, Received ye the Spirit by the works of the law, or by the hearing of faith? Are ye so foolish? having begun in the Spirit, are ye now made perfect by the flesh (Galatians 3:2-3)

While we're discussing Law versus Grace, I'd like us to turn our attention to one of the great theological clichés, that is, "fallen from grace." Contrary to popular belief, you don't "fall from Grace" when you sin. We "fall from grace" when we elect to turn to the law for justification instead of resting in the justification afforded us by the Finished Work of Jesus!

Christ is become of no effect unto you, whosoever of you are justified by the law; ye are fallen from grace. (Galatians 5:4)

If you don't catch anything else here, please catch this – your sin will not cause you to fall from grace or, heaven forbid, lose your salvation!

38

Here's one passage of Scripture that causes legalists and grace abusers alike to cringe – For the legalist, if you're guilty of any part of the Law, you're guilty of the whole. Uphold the tithe but eat bacon for breakfast? Guilty. And for the grace abuser, if you use grace as a license to sin, you place yourself under the purview of the law!

> *But if ye have respect to persons, ye commit sin, and are convinced of the law as transgressors. For whosoever shall keep the whole law, and yet offend in one point, he is guilty of all. For he that said, Do not commit adultery, said also, Do not kill. Now if thou commit no adultery, yet if thou kill, thou art become a transgressor of the law. So speak ye, and so do, as they that shall be judged by the law of liberty (James 2:9-12)*

Moreover, it is impossible to uphold the entire law, that's why Jesus came to fulfill it.

Another of the most misunderstood passages of Scripture – many have taken this to mean you can attain a sinless life in the flesh. If I may, I will present the Scripture and render a proper interpretation:

> *Whosoever committeth sin transgresseth also the law: for sin is the transgression of the law. And ye know that he was manifested to take away our sins; and in him is no sin. Whosoever abideth in him sinneth not:*

whosoever sinneth hath not seen him,
neither known him (1 John 3:4-6)

In Jesus, there is no sin; and Jesus destroyed the spiritual aspect of the sin nature. The "sinneth," here is referring to that sin nature. As you are a new creature in Christ, your sin nature has been put to death. The sin nature cannot abide in Christ and the sin nature cannot see or know God!

The one truth that every believer should catch from all this is that because you are no longer under the Law, you are no longer subject to its bondage and condemnation. You are set free, once and for all. You are no longer a sinner; Jesus makes you righteous, Himself!

There is therefore now no condemnation to them which are in Christ Jesus, who walk not after the flesh, but after the Spirit. For the law of the Spirit of life in Christ Jesus hath made me free from the law of sin and death. For what the law could not do, in that it was weak through the flesh, God sending his own Son in the likeness of sinful flesh, and for sin, condemned sin in the flesh: That the righteousness of the law might be fulfilled in us, who walk not after the flesh, but after the Spirit (Romans 8:1-4)

For he hath made him to be sin for us, who knew no sin; that we might be made the righteousness of God in him. (2 Corinthians 5:21)

40

Jesus is not only the Author and the Finisher of our faith; He is the author and finisher of everything – including the Law!

That, my friends, is Good News!

But the not-so-good-news is that the fruit of the law is a church that is religiously bound to the law.

SIGNS OF A LEGALISTIC CHURCH

Over the past two-thousand years, the church has gone from mere departure to complete distortion of scripture, eschewing the teachings of Jesus, Paul, and the rest of the apostles in favor of man-made doctrines and teachings that have served to hold the people of God in bondage.

Entire movements and denominations have been established to unnecessarily stratify lifestyle constraints and rules, effectively nullifying the grace shed abroad by the blood of Jesus and turning the church from an institution of liberty to a bastion of legalism.

Indeed, these institutions preach sin and hell to the degree that they have become sin-conscious, instead of embracing the righteousness-conscious imparted by the Gospel. As a result, sinful behavior becomes the focus of preaching and discipleship instead righteousness in Christ.

These same institutions preach from the Old Testament with religious fervor, trying to mold New Testament saints into Old Testament paradigms, effectively striving to pour new wine into old wineskins.

The legalist will retort that grace teaching is giving people license to sin and to ignore the "moral law." However, Jesus, Himself, said all the law and the prophets can be distilled to this – Love God and love your neighbor as yourself. And when you get right down to it, the Ten Commandments can be broken down thusly: the first five deal with loving God; the second five deal with loving your neighbor. The legalist will loudly tout the veracity of the Ten Commandments but conveniently exclude the remaining six hundred and three (603). But I digress…

While Paul clearly mentions that the law is holy, righteous, and good, he similarly states with equal clarity that the law does not save us. Moreover, the law is not the measure of righteousness for the NT saint, Christ is (Ephesians 4:11-16). And because He is righteous, so are we (2 Corinthians 5:21)!

The law cannot be our standard because it is impossible to uphold in its entirety (Acts 15:10). While it is the standard by which all non-believers will be judged by, it is most effective when wielded as a tool to show the lost their desperate need for a Savior.

That said, here are the key indicators of a legalistic church:

1. The preachers preach far too many messages on sin and hell.

The wages of sin are death. Period. This is a message that has to be proclaimed FOR THE UNSAVED. However, the gift of God is everlasting life (Romans 6:23)! Jesus instructs us to abide in Him and His Word to abide in us (John 15:4-7) – this joins us to Him. But the Bible also teaches us that in Him there is no sin (1 John 3:5)! Therefore, if we are in Him, we are blameless because we are in Him and in Him there is no sin! It makes no sense to constantly remind saved folks of what they've been saved from! There needs to be more preaching on how to walk in the fullness of Jesus' Finished Work! The Gospel is GOOD NEWS! The Gospel sets people free (2 Corinthians 3:17). Preaching it is far more effective than beating people up over sin and condemning the unsaved to hell.

2. The lead pastor politicizes from the pulpit.

Cultural matters such as abortion and homosexuality, because of codification of perceived sin makes them seemingly easy targets. However, issues such as lying and racism are conveniently ignored. Churches and pastors that strive to legislate from the pulpit ignore the truth that the Kingdom of God is the government that surpasses all governments. Effective Kingdom preaching will break the chains of sin and religion and will displace earthly governments. Don't believe me? Ask the government of Rome!

3. The Old Testament is the standard for holiness and righteousness.

The Old Testament is useful for illustrating the historical basis of the New Covenant. The prophecies of the Old Testament speak not only to the advent of the Messiah but also prophetically to events to come. Others contain eternal wisdom and praise, such as Psalms and Proverbs. And, of course, Genesis, which chapters one and two effectively outline God's mission statement. However, to use the Old Testament as a guide to righteous living serves to put New Testament Saints in bondage. The Old Testament is the chronicling of the Old Covenant and the New Testament is the illustration of the New (Current) Covenant; and the New is superior to the old (Hebrews 8:6-7). Remember, if you're guilty of one point of the law, you're guilty of the whole (James 2:7)!

4. People who live immoral lives are allowed to teach and lead ministries.

Immoral lifestyles are rampant in both legalistic and grace churches. Pulpits and leadership ranks ministries are flush with unbecoming activities. The difference is these matters are conveniently ignored in legalistic churches, lest the musical "anointing" be lost, or the preaching become lifeless, or someone's political boat is rocked; grace churches, on the other hand speak to the individuals in love, allowing the Word of God and the Holy Spirit to effect change. Grace churches are also more likely to teach the correct interpretation of repentance; that is, a change of mind – not confession of sins!

45

5. The lead pastor speaks often against non-institutional church.

The institutional or denominational church is basically a variation of the Roman church, which is a deviation from the first-century church (Acts 2:44-47). Nowhere in the book of Acts do you find the dependence upon hierarchies, devotion to tradition, or being defined by buildings as you do in the modern church. The modern, institutional church has become a corporate machine. It is dependent upon a complex array of talent and resources and has become largely dull to the needs of those lacking said talent and resources. Instead of giving to its community, many institutional churches have become gross consumers of resources.

6. The lead pastor harps on tithing.

There is no New Testament command to tithe. Period. The only cases of tithing before the law was Abraham – who gave tithes of the spoils of war to Melchizedek AND the remainder of the spoil to the King of Sodom – and Jacob – who promised to tithe CONTINGENT UPON God blessing him! There is no evidence of Isaac tithing in Scripture. There is also no evidence of anyone tithing in the New Testament. The paradigm for giving is giving all – understanding that none of it is ours in the first place!

7. The lead pastor only preaches negative messages.

Here's a question: How many times did Jesus preach on hell; how many times did Paul? Why, then, is this a big deal in the modern church? We are called to be preachers of the Gospel; that is, GOOD NEWS. Instead of scaring people to take fire insurance by preaching hell, we should

46

be proclaiming the whole life that is available only in Christ. The only news worth repeating is that God so LOVED the world that He sent His Son to be not only the payment for our sin that we may have ETERNAL life (John 3:16), but that we should have abundant life in the here-and-now (John 10:10). The key to grace teaching is the Greek word, "sozo," which not only means salvation from sin but also deliverance from demonic oppression, bodily healing, and material blessing. The legalistic church and its preachers will tell you that prosperity is not for the believer, healing died with the original Apostles, and that deliverance is completely dependent upon the oppressed. Folks, that ain't good news!

There are many other things I could mention regarding legalistic churches and their preaching – like how they are one step away from Calvinism (that only the "elite elect" are saved and everyone else is born to go to hell) and traditions of men that nullify the Word of God (Mark 7:13), because many of their traditions have little basis in the Word. It's time to get away from the traditions and religion that have shackled the Body of Christ for centuries and get back to the bold simplicity preached by Jesus and His Apostles.

To be clear, Grace is not the license to sin, it is liberation from the yoke of sin.

The legalistic church is the nest of the traditions of men – those traditions that have little to no basis in Scripture.

TRADITIONS OF MEN

God framed the heavens and the earth with His Words. With His Word, He created the spirit of man. By His Word, God made His Word flesh. In His Word are salvation, deliverance, healing, protection, and prosperity. We must conclude, therefore, that God's Word is powerful. And yet, there is something so nullifying, so negating that even Jesus said renders this Word of no effect.

The traditions of men nullify the Word of God.

Don't take my word for it, check out what Jesus had to say about this:

Making the word of God of none effect through your tradition, which ye have delivered: and many such like things do ye. (Mark 7:13)

Christians are longing for the power of God to be manifest in their lives and churches and they long to see this power expressed in their services and congregations – but the power of God will not overrun the traditions of men.

Notice here I said, "will not," not "cannot." You see, God is omnipotent; He can do anything but lie or fail. But God never forces His will on man. He could easily force us to bow down and worship Him. Yet, He never does, as that would be contrary to His character. God is the archetypal gentleman!

Back to my point, there are so many churches that are steeped in denominationalism and rooted in tradition that they end up ignoring Scripture. I know that there are many churches that will not permit me to preach in their pulpits because of my long, dreadlocked hair. I know of others that will not permit women to preach to their congregations. Still more would exclude many a potential guest preacher because of race or culture. These traditions are based upon errant interpretation of Scripture that I have neither the time nor space to correct.

(By the way, this exclusion based on tradition cheats many from hearing from anointed preachers and teachers…)

Tradition often paints an inaccurate portrait of the Church and Kingdom Citizens. Mahatma Gandhi once said he'd have become a Christian had he never met one.

What an indictment against the Church!

Today, folks stay away from church by the thousands, citing hypocrisy, mean-spiritedness, and other factors – most stemming from tradition. Because tradition renders powerless the Word of God, there are no signs and wonders displayed for the purpose of winning the lost. Traditions of men are what largely keep folks from experiencing the beauty of relationship with the Father through Jesus.

Many churches are so yoked to liturgy that a move of the Holy Spirit is nigh impossible. The stated program must be followed. Proper protocol must be observed. Many believers have been thoroughly convinced that their style of worship, their hymns, and their atmosphere is the only way to approach God. Others insist that proper dress is important – men must wear suits to worship and women cannot wear pants, and so forth. Let any of these elements be out of place and congregations that have become reliant, indeed, dependent upon tradition will become non-functional, complementing their dysfunction.

Now, the Bible teaches us that God esteems His Word above His Name (Psalm 138:2). The Pharisees evoked Jesus' anger by esteeming tradition over the Word and folks today have the audacity to follow in their footsteps. By continuing this folly, the very power, yes, the nature of God is not expressed fully to His children.

Instead of obsessing over meaningless traditions that are devoid of power, we need to focus on the Word of God to the end of manifesting the Greater Works Jesus spoke of in John 14:12. Instead of practicing hollow worship smacking of man's tradition, we need to go forth and fulfill the Great Commission – that is, preaching God's unconditional Love and Grace and making disciples (Mark 16:15)

It's time to put away denominational dogma that hinder winning of the lost and properly discipling the saints. It will be a glorious day in the Kingdom when the yokes of tradition and the bondage of defiled religion are destroyed once and for all.

Traditions, unchecked, become dogmatic. Once they become dogma, the power of God becomes ineffective. Once the power of God becomes ineffective, you get a product theologians call "cessationism."

THE STRANGE FIRE OF CESSATIONISM

T here's a great deal of discussion around the Biblical term, "Strange Fire." The implications of this commotion are that there is much in the Body of Christ that is tantamount to improper worship; worship that God is not pleased with.

The connotation of "Strange Fire" is rooted in the railing against the broad spectrum of modern Christianity called the "Charismatic Movement." This is construed to include – but not limited to – "Word of Faith," "Prosperity," and "Pentecostal Healing/Delivery" ministries. Now, I'd understand if the focus was on the shortcomings of these ministries but there seems to be a stake-in-the-ground stance that decries Charismatic ministries, *en toto*.

There have been many failings in the Charismatic Movement. A myriad of improprieties have dogged many ministries. However, it is unfair to paint these ministries with a broad-brush, as the same failings have occurred in orthodox, traditional ministries as well.

Before moving forward, let's take a look at what the Bible has to say about "Strange Fire:"

> *And Nadab and Abihu, the sons of Aaron, took either of them his censer, and put fire therein, and put incense thereon, and offered strange fire before the Lord, which he commanded them not. And there went out fire from the Lord, and devoured them, and they died before the Lord. (Leviticus 10:1)*

> *And Nadab and Abihu died before the Lord, when they offered strange fire before the Lord, in the wilderness of Sinai, and they had no children: and Eleazar and Ithamar ministered in the priest's office in the sight of Aaron their father. (Numbers 3:4)*

And Nadab and Abihu died, when they offered strange fire before the Lord. (Numbers 26:61)

The Biblical definition of "Strange Fire," then, would appear to be fire that is kindled against the instruction of the Lord or an unpleasing sacrifice to God.

There is also a term tossed about in Christian circles that "fire always falls on sacrifice." Here is the source of that:

> *Then the fire of the Lord fell, and consumed the burnt sacrifice, and the wood, and the stones, and the dust, and licked up the water that was in the trench. (1 Kings 18:38)*

In each of these cases, there was a sacrifice made unto the Lord by men. And, in each of these cases, the occurrence was before the dispensation of Grace under the New Covenant.

Isaiah saw the plan of God clearly when he wrote the following:

> *But he was wounded for our transgressions, he was bruised for our iniquities: the chastisement of our peace was upon him; and with his stripes we are healed. (Isaiah 53:5)*

In other words, the punishment that was fit for every man living under the curse of sin was laid upon Jesus. He was perfectly God and perfectly man; therefore He became the perfect sacrifice – or propitiation – for the sins of mankind. Jesus blotted out the ordinances of the law, fulfilling them by His perfect sacrifice.

In Jesus, the fire has fallen – once and for all – on His sacrifice.

Therefore, God is not raining down fire to punish anyone. What God will do in the earth is rebuke according to His Word (2 Timothy 3:16).

Speaking of rebuke, there is a "Strange Fire" mentioned in the New Testament:

> *And when his disciples James and John saw this, they said, Lord, wilt thou that we command fire to come down from heaven, and consume them, even as Elias did? (Luke 9:54)*

Sadly, this is the kind of "Strange Fire" that persists today – a terrorist spirit that provokes God to rain down judgment upon all who are in disagreement with it. It's "Strange," indeed, that entire conferences are dedicated to decrying opposing thought – instead of pursuing a Kingdom mandate to win the lost of the world and to disciple the Saints. Jesus countered with a strong rebuke:

> *But he turned, and rebuked them, and said, Ye know not what manner of spirit ye are of. For the Son of man is not come to destroy men's lives, but to save them. And they went to another village. (Luke 9:55-56)*

In Jesus' eyes, the "Strange Fire" we need to be concerned with is that which men would use to destroy other men. The "Strange Fire" of today holds that miracles have ceased and that those who desire or manifest them are operating against God's will and His Word.

Nothing could be further from the truth. Again, we need to consider the Words of Jesus:

> *And John answered him, saying, Master, we saw one casting out devils in thy name, and he followeth not us: and we forbad him, because he followeth not us. But Jesus said, Forbid him not: for there is no man which shall do a miracle in my name, that can lightly speak evil of me. For he that is not against us is on our part. (Mark 9:38-40)*

At the end-of-the-day, pointing out "Strange Fire" indicates a fear of what runs contrary to the established traditional, religious system. Instead of trying to decry and cower away from the Charismatic movement, traditional Christianity would do well to embrace the Words of the Lord and not strive to browbeat those who are different than them – but not against them.

If the teaching you hear purports to represent Christ but is devoid of the Love of God and Liberty in Christ – and fails to reveal the fullness of the Kingdom of God – it is, indeed, "Strange Fire."

THE FAILURE OF DENOMINATIONS

Some denominations with feigned holiness and contrived righteousness that have a form of godliness but deny the power thereof really need to be either reformed wholesale or scrapped altogether. We need to move away every obstacle to make Jesus plain and visible to even the casual observer.

Jesus said that the traditions of men make of none effect the Word of God (Mark 7:13). Pause and think about that: the very Word that created all things (Genesis 1) and upholds all things (Hebrews 1:3) is essentially nullified by what man doggedly clings to in lieu of what is prescribed by scripture.

So, things such as: no women pastors, women can't wear pants, men can't wear long hair, men can't wear earrings, women can't wear open-toed shoes, women can't wear makeup, today's preachers are the modern-day Levitical priesthood, etcetera, are all vain traditions of men that are not Scriptural and should be scrapped.

The question of the day, then, is: why are Christians so determined to hang on to traditions that are clearly unscriptural? And why, then, do they wonder why they operate in complete powerlessness.

There are over 41,000 Christian denominations in the world. How did this happen? It likely began with the split between the Catholic and Eastern Orthodox churches. Some will say it was an outgrowth of the Protestant Reformation, started by Martin Luther. Others will contend that further schisms grew from the Welsh revival. Still more can be ascribed to the Azusa Street revival. Indeed, there is truth to all of these. And every denomination (including "non-denominational) has a common denominator:

All of them believe they are correct.

Jesus clearly said, "I am THE WAY, THE TRUTH, and THE LIFE; No man cometh unto the Father BUT BY ME" (John 14:6). Sounds pretty simple, right? However, over time, folks have added their take on how Jesus should be presented and how His Word should be interpreted.

And, as a result, we now have layer-upon-layer of extra-Scriptural doctrine, things that have absolutely nothing to do with Christ – or even Christianity.

There are two simple formulas that will tell you if what is being preached or taught is authentic:

Jesus + nothing = everything

And…

Jesus + anything = nothing

In other words, we shouldn't be adding anything to the Gospel. When you try to add to the simplicity of the Gospel message, it becomes both tainted and complicated.

What is needed in the Body of Christ is a return to the ministry model given in Ephesians 4. This will take us back to the simplicity of Scripture and also go a long way toward returning the power that is desperately needed in the Church. What power? The same sick-healing, dead-raising, demon-bashing power that was demonstrated by Jesus!

Ephesians 4:11-14 tells us what the purpose of ministry gifts truly are. Let's take a walk through this seminal passage of scripture:

11 And he gave some, apostles; and some, prophets; and some, evangelists; and some, pastors and teachers;

These are the ministry gifts given by God to ensure that His Word is effectively preached and practiced in the world.

12 For the perfecting of the saints, for the work of the ministry, for the edifying of the body of Christ:

The word, "perfecting" is rendered thusly in Strong's:

g2677. καταρτισμός katartismos; from 2675; complete furnishing (objectively):– perfecting.
AV (1)– perfecting 1; complete furnishing, equipping

Which means that the purpose of ministry is to equip the saints to do the work of the ministry – which brings about the first of three salient questions:

Question 1.) Is denominational ministry equipping the saints? Jesus told us that greater works we would do because He went unto His Father (John 14:12). Are the works that Jesus did being done in greater number? Then the answer to this question is, "no."

13 Till we all come in the unity of the faith, and of the knowledge of the Son of God,

60

*unto a perfect man, unto the measure of the
stature of the fulness of Christ:*

The words, "unity," "faith," and "knowledge" are thus
rendered by Strong's:

> **g1775**. *ἑνότης henotēs; from 1520; oneness,
> i. e. (figuratively) unanimity:– unity.
> AV (2)– unity 2; unity unanimity, agreement*

Question 2.) Has the Body of Christ come to unity of
faith? No. Have we come to the full knowledge of Jesus
and the stature of the fullness of Christ? Nope. The mere
fact that we have denominations in the abundance we do
is indicative of the lack of unity in the Body of Christ.

> **g4102**. *πίστις pistis; from 3982; persuasion,
> i. e. credence; moral conviction (of
> religious truth, or the truthfulness of God or
> a religious teacher), especially reliance
> upon Christ for salvation; abstractly,
> constancy in such profession; by extension,
> the system of religious (Gospel) truth itself:
> – assurance, belief, believe, faith, fidelity.
> AV (244)– faith 239, assurance 1, believe
> + g1537 1, belief 1, them that believe 1,
> fidelity 1; conviction of the truth of anything,
> belief; in the NT of a conviction or belief
> respecting man's relationship to God and
> divine things, generally with the included
> idea of trust and holy fervour born of faith
> and joined with it relating to God the
> conviction that God exists and is the creator*

61

and ruler of all things, the provider and bestower of eternal salvation through Christ relating to Christ a strong and welcome conviction or belief that Jesus is the Messiah, through whom we obtain eternal salvation in the kingdom of God the religious beliefs of Christians belief with the predominate idea of trust (or confidence) whether in God or in Christ, springing from faith in the same fidelity, faithfulness the character of one who can be relied on

The fact that healing and deliverance are not prevalent in the Body of Christ is proof that faith is lacking individually, much less group-wise.

g1922. ἐπίγνωσις epignōsis; from 1921; recognition, i. e. (by implication) full discernment, acknowledgement:– (ac-) knowledge (– ing,– ment).
AV (20)– knowledge 16, acknowledging 3, acknowledgement 1;
precise and correct knowledge used in the NT of the knowledge of things ethical and divine

Question 3:) Are we anchored in Biblical doctrine, or are we moved by every perceived "move of God?" I think more of the latter and less of the former.

14 That we henceforth be no more children, tossed to and fro, and carried about with every wind of doctrine, by the sleight of men,

and cunning craftiness, whereby they lie in
wait to deceive;

Truth of the matter, most denominations are completely impotent when it comes to discipleship.

The beginning of unity in the Body of Christ is at the end of denominationalism. And the first step toward tearing down denominational walls is the understanding of what ministry gifts are…and are not.

MINISTRY GIFTS

Romans 11:29 declares, "For the gifts and calling of God are without repentance." That said, man cannot deem the office of the Apostle is no more. Ephesians 4:11 says the Lord "...GAVE some, apostles; and some, prophets; and some, evangelists; and some, pastors and teachers;" Please note that He GAVE — that means these offices are GIFTS from God!

These gifts also have a purpose, illustrated in Ephesians 4:12, "for the perfecting (or equipping) of the saints for the work of the ministry, for the edifying of the body of Christ:" We must therefore ask the question, Have the saints been fully equipped? The answer to that question, clearly, is, "no."

And they have a time limit, shown in Ephesians 4:13,

...Till we all come in the unity of the faith, and of the knowledge of the Son of God, unto a perfect man, unto the measure of the stature of the fulness of Christ:"

We are compelled to ask again, "Is the Body of Christ operating in unity?" The answer, sadly, is, "no."

1 Corinthians 12:28 tells us "And God hath set some in the church, first apostles, secondarily prophets, thirdly teachers, after that miracles, then gifts of healings, helps, governments, diversities of tongues." Note, here, the Apostle Paul says "in the church." Since we are in the church era, this pertains to the "here-and-now."

Now each office is unique -- interdependent in the body yet independent in function. Neither is any greater than the other. You need not first become a Bishop before becoming an Apostle; no more than one need be an Evangelist before becoming a Pastor.

Concerning the office of the Bishop, Strong's renders it thusly:

g1984. *ἐπισκοπή episkopē; from 1980; inspection (for relief); by implication, superintendence; specially, the Christian "episcopate": – the office of a "bishop",* *bishoprick, visitation. AV (4)– visitation 2, bishoprick 1, office of a bishop 1; Investigation, inspection, visitation that act by which God looks into and searches out the ways, deeds character, of men, in order to adjudge them their lot accordingly, whether joyous or sad oversight overseership, office, charge, the office of an elder the overseer or presiding officers of a Christian church*

In other words, the Bishop is a superintendent or overseer. In modern parlance, the Bishop is what might be referred to as a Pastor to pastors. A Bishop is, therefore, a Pastor but not all Pastors are Bishops.

While these matters are, indeed, important to Church governance, I think they pale compared to the weightier matters of soul-winning and discipling. We must understand the offices of leadership are gifts to the Body of Christ but know that these gifts are not for the benefit of those who operate within them but for the Church and its edification. We must be faithful to that which makes disciples, matures believers and multiplies ministries.

The misunderstanding of the ministry gifts has lead to the erection of needless, man-made hierarchies.

RELIGION AND HIERARCHIES

A funny thing happened between the first-century church and the modern church. Somehow, a simple idea comprised of Jesus Christ and those who willingly chose to be discipled after him got complicated into a convoluted mess of hierarchy.

From the time Jesus walked the earth to the time of the first-century church, there was no hierarchy. Jesus was the head and everyone else was equal under Him.

In fact, in order to gather any evidence supporting hierarchy, you have to go outside Scripture. And, unfortunately, there are tons of documentation that are used to support this – too many, in fact, to go over here.

Leadership is not putting people under your authority; rather, it is going out in front of people as a scout or guide. It isn't delegating dirty work to underlings; it is doing the heavy lifting and showing people how things should be done.

To understand whether hierarchies should be observed, we need to see what Jesus' take on them was:

> *Then came to him the mother of Zebedee's children with her sons, worshipping him, and desiring a certain thing of him. And he said unto her, What wilt thou? She saith unto him, Grant that these my two sons may sit, the one on thy right hand, and the other on the left, in thy kingdom. But Jesus answered and said, Ye know not what ye ask. Are ye able to drink of the cup that I shall drink of, and to be baptized with the baptism that I am baptized with? They say unto him, We are able. And he saith unto them, Ye shall drink indeed of my cup, and be baptized with the baptism that I am baptized with: but to sit on my right hand, and on my left, is not mine to give, but it shall be given to them for whom it is prepared of my Father. (Matthew 20:20-24)*

Here, Jesus was challenged by the mother of James and John to place her sons at the top of His Kingdom hierarchy. Jesus responded by saying that hierarchy was for the Father to give. Jesus said in John 14:9 that those who have seen Him have seen the Father. And, yet, the very image of the Father revealed nothing of hierarchy.

It was always God's plan that all of mankind would be equal. The Apostle Paul put it thusly:

> *There is neither Jew nor Greek, there is neither bond nor free, there is neither male nor female: for ye are all one in Christ Jesus. (Galatians 3:28)*

Simply put, all are equal in Christ. He is the Head and we are His Body!

The Pharisees and Sadducees were stuck on religious hierarchies. In fact, they were stuck on religion, period. Jesus came to tear down their religion and their hierarchies.

> *Tend the flock of God which is among you, exercising the oversight, not of constraint, but willingly, according to the will of God; nor yet for filthy lucre, but of a ready mind; neither as lording it over the charge allotted to you, but making yourselves ensamples to the flock. (1 Peter 5:2-3)*

> *But Jesus called them unto him, and said, Ye know that the princes of the Gentiles exercise dominion over them, and they that are great exercise authority upon them. But it shall not be so among you: but whosoever*

will be great among you, let him be your
minister; And whosoever will be chief
among you, let him be your servant: Even as
the Son of man came not to be ministered
unto, but to minister, and to give his life a
ransom for many. (Matthew 20:25-28)

When God gave man dominion in the earth (Genesis 1:26-28), it was for man to have authority over his environment and his circumstances, not other men. When men misappropriate dominion, abuses of authority are inevitable.

COVERING

O f the many topics covered in this book there are few that will raise more eyebrows than the concept of "covering." As a Pastor and a Bishop, this topic comes up in my circles with increasing frequency. I have been asked who is my covering and, also, whom do I cover?

The short answers are, the Holy Spirit and no one.

I've thrown down this gauntlet before and, for the sake of this tome, I will do it again:

Where, exactly, is the concept or principle of "covering" elucidated in scripture? My contention is that it is not.

Why, then, is it such a big deal? And what exactly is "covering?" To cover something means to hide or conceal it, or to protect it. There is no man that can hide me from the devil, much less God. Similarly, there is no man who can protect me more than the Holy Spirit who dwells within me. So, what's the point?

I have come to the conclusion that those who subscribe to the notion of "covering" err out of either omission or commission.

The omission camp garners more of my sympathy. These are the folks who do it a certain way because "that's the way we've always done it." Generally, this is the band whose heart is in the right place. They highly venerate tradition and eschew "rocking the boat," as they say to avoid offending those of like minds. At the risk of suggesting these folks don't know better, they truly don't. "Covering," for them, is the way of continuing their denomination and preserving the discipline of the pulpit. They blissfully ignore the fact that covering is nowhere in scripture, sticking instead to the tenets of denominational doctrine.

The commission camp, on the other hand, gleans far less sympathy from me. These are the folks who know better and refuse to do better. This is the group that has revelation but uses it for the purpose of manipulation. "Covering" in this context is very lucrative, as control is exercised over new initiates into the ministry to regulate what they preach and teach, extending that control to financial matters.

"Covering," here, insists that "spiritual sons" bear the burden of financially supporting "spiritual fathers." This band knows covering isn't at all scriptural but aims to loosely cobble together Scripture for the purpose of justifying their premise.

An error, by omission or commission, is still an error and, thus, requires correction. Both camps are in error but the former must be led to the truth in love, whereas the latter will only come to the truth kicking and screaming.

Now, the concept of spiritual fathers/spiritual sons is, indeed, scriptural but this relationship has been skewed for base gain. Many spiritual fathers draw from the models of both earthly fathers and our Heavenly Father in that they bear the responsibility for the care and instruction of their spiritual sons in the same manner that an earthly father would. That is, earthly fathers provide support and a "covering" for their wife and children – and the children only until they come of age.

Where it gets twisted, though, is when spiritual sons financially support spiritual fathers. In the natural, such a father would be regarded as both coercive and abusive but this is considered to be "normal" in ministry. Equally abusive is when spiritual sons are expected to be clones of their spiritual fathers – even to the point of not doing the prayer and study required of sermon preparation; opting, instead, to parrot the sermons of the spiritual father.

Some may say, "Well, Preacher, what about accountability; isn't that what 'covering' is all about?" To that inquiry, I point to the book of Acts – all the apostles were on one accord, equal in responsibility, and accountable to one another under the headship of the Lord Jesus.

The concept of "covering" is one of the typical trappings of vain religion. Covenant, on the other hand, is Biblically supported. True ministry relationships are covenant-based.

To further illuminate, a covenant – simply defined – is when two parties enter into agreement to put their resources and relationship at one another's disposal and to protect one another's resources and reputation.

In discussing ministerial relationships, I would be remiss in my duties if I ignore one of the "third-rail" subjects of church leadership, that is, women in ministry. If you're still with me, hang on…

WOMEN IN MINISTRY

One of the great follies in Christianity is the tendency to take a situational text and build a doctrine around it. When this happens, religion builds a stronghold that rivals anything the devil or our thought lives can construct. In another chapter, I explain how religion uses Scripture on tithing to hold Saints in bondage, because there is no New Testament command to tithe. In this chapter, though, I want to deal with something equally constraining:

The prohibition of Women in Ministry.

Over centuries, a general patriarchy was constructed that reduced women to second-class citizens. Women were reduced to servitude; their intellect and ability either muted or underutilized. Nowhere in history is this truer than in the church.

Yeah, the "Christian" church. The one founded by Jesus and spread by His Apostles.

Before we get too far down the path, let's establish a Scriptural baseline:

> *26 For ye are all the children of God by faith in Christ Jesus. 27 For as many of you as have been baptized into Christ have put on Christ. 28 There is neither Jew nor Greek, there is neither bond nor free, there is neither male nor female: for ye are all one in Christ Jesus. 29 And if ye be Christ's, then are ye Abraham's seed, and heirs according to the promise. (Galatians 3:26-29)*

We see, here, that Paul is speaking of a general baseline or anti-hierarchy in Christ. All are equal in the Kingdom of God. If only all of Christendom could hang their collective hat here, there would be no need for this chapter!

The Gospel is Good News. In fact, that word "Gospel" is not a mere descriptive, it is a hyperbole – it literally means "too-good-to-be-true news!" But, as it is with so many things mankind puts its hand to, something always gets twisted, like wicker furniture and baskets; wicker and wicked have the same etymology!

Here is the key Scripture that is most commonly taken out of context:

> *34 Let your women keep silence in the churches: for it is not permitted unto them to speak; but they are commanded to be under obedience, as also saith the law. 35 And if they will learn any thing, let them ask their husbands at home: for it is a shame for women to speak in the church.* (1 Corinthians 14:34-35)

First and foremost, context must be considered. Three questions must be submitted: 1) to whom was Paul speaking? 2) What was he addressing? And 3) what was the cultural and societal climate?

Paul was speaking specifically to the church at Corinth. He was addressing the issue plaguing Corinthian society, that is, women dominating men. No more than men should dominate women, Paul was addressing an issue of societal imbalance prevalent in Corinthian culture that was creeping into the young church.

Okay, that's really two answers to three questions – but I hope you catch my point.

There is a reason Paul teaches us to bring every thought into captivity (2 Corinthians 10:5) – good or bad – because every thought without godly reference becomes a brick in the aforementioned stronghold. This is one of those cases.

What has happened is that a text Paul wrote as a rebuke to a particular church over a particular matter has taken on a life of its own, and become the basis of a – dare I say – demonic doctrine.

Because religion has ignored the broader context and used this to quench the spiritual fire of God-only-knows how many women, the church has failed to come up to the standard of maturity referenced in Ephesians 4:13-15. How can the ministry gifts be fully expressed (Ephesians 4:11-12) when possibly more than half of those through whom the Lord gave those gifts are ignored or silenced?

Of course, those who abide by the old chestnut of "no woman preachers" will likely trot out:

> *But I suffer not a woman to teach, nor to*
> *usurp authority over the man, but to be in*
> *silence. (1 Timothy 2:12)*

This, too, is contextual. Paul wrote this epistle to Timothy who, at the time of the writing, was in Ephesus. At the time, the Ephesian church was dealing with the infection of pagan teaching, including the same goddess worship that caused the women in Corinth to usurp the authority of men.

Let's take a look at how women were used throughout the Bible. First of all, you had Rahab, a harlot who had the sense enough to know that God was greater than the "gods" worshiped in Jericho (Joshua 2:8-13). Rahab was regarded so highly by God that the lineage that brought forth both David and Jesus was birthed through her.

Then, there was Deborah, who was a mighty prophetess and judge over Israel. She was also a mighty warrior, who helped win a decisive victory over Sisera and the king of the Canaanites (Judges 4).

Next was the unnamed woman at the well. Upon hearing Jesus' Words, she left what she came to do to preach the Gospel of the Kingdom to the people of Samaria. Now, don't go get your knickers in a knot over this, let's go to the Word and see this for ourselves:

> *39 And many of the Samaritans of that city believed on him for the saying of the woman, which testified, He told me all that ever I did. 40 So when the Samaritans were come unto him, they besought him that he would tarry with them: and he abode there two days. 41 And many more believed because of his own word; 42 And said unto the woman, Now we believe, not because of thy saying: for we have heard him ourselves, and know that this is indeed the Christ, the Saviour of the world (John 4:39-42).*

Do you see that – she preached and they believed. She took the Gospel of the Kingdom to people shunned by the Jews and they came to believe!

But I ain't done yet…

There's Mary, the sister of Martha and Lazarus. We find her sitting at the feet of Jesus (Luke 10:38-39), a very privileged position reserved for His disciples. She wanted to hear the Word while her sister was obsessed with serving.

Next we have Mary Magdalene. We see her at the temporary burial place of Jesus when she encounters the risen Savior. Her case is special because she was the first person to proclaim (preach) the resurrection. If you have a little trouble downloading this truth, let me help you with Scripture:

> *Jesus saith unto her, Touch me not; for I am not yet ascended to my Father: but go to my brethren, and say unto them, I ascend unto my Father, and your Father; and to my God, and your God. Mary Magdalene came and told the disciples that she had seen the Lord, and that he had spoken these things unto her. (John 20:17:18)*

When Jesus says, "go," we can safely conclude it's not a suggestion but a command! And she was sent, like the twelve in Luke 9 and the seventy-two in Luke 10. The command, "go," is an implied ordination – in other words, she was given an assignment and she faithfully executed it!

That one alone should destroy the yoke of bad doctrine prohibiting women from serving in ministry. However, if you're still not convinced, there is, as they say, still more!

Let's have a look at Priscilla, the wife of Aquila. She, along with her husband discipled Apollos, who later became an Apostle (Acts 18:24-26). Paul referred to Priscilla and Aquila as his helpers in Christ Jesus and made mention of the church in their home (Romans 16:3). Paul was also fond of them as they labored together in the occupation of tentmaking.

Finally, we see that there was a woman by the name of Junia who, along with her husband Andronicus was not only imprisoned with Paul, She was referred to as a noteworthy Apostle (Romans 16:7).

I'm reminded of an anecdote recounted by an old Deacon in East Texas regarding his daughter, who is a pastor of a growing ministry. I think this story will help put this chapter in perspective.

"Daddy, God called me to preach." His reply, "Oh Lawd!"

That night, God took the ol' Deacon back to his childhood in a dream. On their farm, they had a reliable rooster that would crow on time every day. Well one day, that old rooster up and died.

Now, if you know anything about chickens, you know a good rooster is hard to find. So, during the search for a new rooster, one of the hens jumped up on a fence post and began crowing like the rooster did, and did so until they got another rooster.

The Spirit of the Lord asked Deke if he ever cursed that hen for crowing, and Deke said, "no…"

The Spirit continued, "Then don't curse your daughter."

The Deacon's daughter pastors a thriving church …with her Daddy's blessings.

True story…

I pray this chapter will – once and for all – tear down the stronghold against women in ministry. I believe that once all the patriarchal sensibilities have been laid to rest, we will see the ministry gifts expand and the Church grow to the fullness of stature and maturity in Christ, and bear the fruit that is evidence of the life-giving True Vine. If there is neither the love of God nor Liberty in Christ in either message or doctrine, you can safely conclude that message or doctrine is not from God. You will find neither of these key indicators in the doctrine that forbids women from preaching, pastoring, or otherwise leading. Prohibiting women from serving in ministry is, therefore, a godless doctrine.

What discussion of church would be complete without a discussion of praise and worship?

PRAISE AND WORSHIP

If you're like most Christians, these two words will lead you to thoughts of music. For the purposes of this book, though, I'd like to take a look at these in a more esoteric fashion.

The first time we see the word "praise" in Scripture is when Leah gives birth to her fourth son, Judah:

> 35 And she conceived again, and bare a son: and she said, Now will I praise the Lord: therefore she called his name Judah; and left bearing. (Genesis 29:35 KJV)

Judah is the patriarch of the tribe through whom Jesus comes from and his name, literally, means, "praised."

Since Jesus is the object of our praise, it is fitting that He spring from this lineage.

More on that in a minute...

The first time we encounter "worship" in Scripture is the account of Abraham preparing to sacrifice Isaac:

> *5 And Abraham said unto his young men, Abide ye here with the ass; and I and the lad will go yonder and worship, and come again to you. (Genesis 22:5 KJV)*

It is noteworthy that the first mention of "worship" comes in context with the first mention of the word, "love:"

> *2 And he said, Take now thy son, thine only son Isaac, whom thou lovest, and get thee into the land of Moriah; and offer him there for a burnt offering upon one of the mountains which I will tell thee of. (Genesis 22:2 KJV)*

It's pretty clear that love and worship go together because worship is a form of affection. Worship is a synonym for "adoration." A child loves her parents and, indeed, worships them. Husbands and wives render a form of worship to one another. Worship is a byproduct of love. And before you get all twisted up about this, God gave commands about worshiping other "gods." Something or someone who demands obedience is by definition, a "god." Ascribing godlike qualities to someone or something unworthy of such is idolatry – i.e., you can make an idol out of anything.

And, typically, we render praise to anyone or anything that has proven themselves/itself reliable, trustworthy, or even lovable.

But I digress…

Jesus is God – He is the Word (God's creative and communicative power) made flesh. We worship Him because He loves us and we love Him. We praise Him because He is good.

In other words, neither praise nor worship are religious exercises.

I like to think that before time began – or before "start" "started" – God was God, sitting in heaven, being God. And because He is God, he is holy – that is, whole, complete, nothing lacking. And He was thinking to Himself, "I'm so good, I think I'll reproduce myself." Now, God certainly didn't *need* to reproduce Himself. He did it because He wanted to.

God did it because He was so full of Love.

So, when God reproduced Himself in man, He established a relationship with Him. I think it's interesting that in creation, you find none of the trappings of religion. There are no altars, no priests, no temples, and no robes.

That's because true worship only comes from relationship. Only what is loved can be truly worshiped. If you worship out of fear of retribution, it isn't truly worship.

And you can only truly praise that which is praiseworthy. If you praise something or someone who or which is lacking in this quality, it is hollow praise.

Contrary to popular belief, we are not created to worship or to praise God. While I'm sure God delights in our praising and worshiping Him, I'm equally sure that He will continue to be more that content in His identity and being whether we praise and worship Him or not. People can be addicted to praise (Praise addiction disorder) but I think God is much bigger and far more secure than that.

Praise and worship are not things we do; they are characteristics of who we are in Christ. Unfortunately, religion has conditioned people to become conditioned – or even addicted – to performing them.

Religion demands performance and the bigger, the better. When we shout louder, we believe praise and worship is intensified. When we sing and dance longer, praise and worship is believed to be more effective. In other words, the more we do and the more fervently we do it, we are conditioned to believe that it is more acceptable to God.

But performance was never what it was about.

When we fast-forward into redemption, beginning with the advent of Jesus' earthly ministry, we see Jesus receiving worship but He admonishes the religious zealots for religious vanity:

> *8 This people draweth nigh unto me with their mouth, and honoureth me with their*

lips; but their heart is far from me. 9 But in vain they do worship me, teaching for doctrines the commandments of men. (Matthew 15:8-9 KJV)

However, Jesus made no demands for worship. We see people praising Jesus for what He has done for them, but he doesn't make this a prerequisite for his manifestation of the miraculous. In the cases of both worship and praise, we see it as a flowing toward him because of relationship with Him.

Jesus, then, takes this and makes it scandalous. He takes religion out of the picture entirely by portraying God first as *His* Father but then as *Our* Father. He shows us the true path to worship by reconciliation and restoration. He makes Himself the praise by telling us that we pray to (communicate with) the Father in His Name.

God, and God alone, must be the object of our worship and the focus of our praise. Unfortunately, religion has created a culture of worshiping worship. And when we worship "worship," we often fall into the trap of worshiping the place of worship.

THE SANCTUARY

When we look at Scripture we find two overarching concepts, creation and redemption.

Every Sunday morning, much ado will be made about being in the "House of God." More specifically, people will talk about how wonderful it is to be "in the Sanctuary" and how we must labor with our efforts and our money to keep "the Sanctuary."

Indeed, a lot of emphasis is placed on physical "places of worship." This sounds spiritual and holy but it is terribly misguided.

If you'll spare me a few moments, I'd like to talk about the "sanctuary." Let's start by taking a look at some words of Paul that are obvious to this discussion and some words of Jesus that would not seem so:

19 Do you not know that your body is the temple (the very sanctuary) of the Holy Spirit Who lives within you, Whom you have received [as a Gift] from God? You are not your own, 20 You were bought with a price [purchased with a preciousness and paid for, made His own]. So then, honor God and bring glory to Him in your body (1 Corinthians 6:19-20 AMP)

For the Son of Man came to seek and to save that which was lost. (Luke 19:10 AMP)

The first thing we see is Paul telling us that the true sanctuary of God is not buildings made with the hands of men but the hearts of men made by the hands of God. We were purchased with the Blood of Jesus to become part of the family of God and the dwelling place of the Spirit of God.

It was never God's intention to dwell in buildings. When God created man, He breathed His life into us. He gave us his appearance, the ability to think and speak, and His essence. God created the earth to be the dwelling place of His dwelling place!

One of the follies of religion is that it tries to craft its own way of reaching God. The first instance of this is the construction of the tower of Babel (Genesis 11:1-9). In this account, the people all came together with a singular purpose – to build an edifice to reach God. In other words, the people were trying to reach God on their own terms. This is the first appearance of religion in recorded history.

We know how that turned out.

Another thing to consider is what theologians call "creative intent." Nowhere in the creation account is there a "place of worship." If places of worship were so important to God, surely He'd have established one with the man He originally created, right?

Fast forward to David. David was a man after God's own heart (1 Samuel 13:14). David loved God and was the first man after Adam to catch a glimpse of God as Father (Psalms 68:5, 89:26). He wrote in Psalms that He wanted to dwell in the house of God:

> *(Psalms 27:4 KJV) One thing have I desired of the Lord, that will I seek after; that I may dwell in the house of the Lord all the days of my life, to behold the beauty of the Lord, and to enquire in his temple.*

David caught the heart of God – it was God who wanted to dwell in His people!

David wanted to build a temple for God but God passed that responsibility to David's son, Solomon. Solomon did, indeed build the temple but, eventually, the people placed more emphasis on the temple instead of its Tenant. This caused the people to veer from the precepts of God, which led to centuries of captivity.

In the Old Testament, it was said that God inhabited the praises of His people (Psalm 22:3). But thanks be to Jesus, God now inhabits us (Romans 8:11)!

Now on to what Jesus said – and while this is not so obvious it is absolutely powerful.

When He said He came to seek and to save that which was lost, we need to look at the pronoun, "that." This word is an impersonal pronoun, so it can't be pertaining to people. However, some translators have rendered the "that" as "those," thus making it a personal pronoun pertaining to people.

So how is this reconciled? I prayerfully asked this question for a long time and God spoke to me in a dream, telling me "sanctuary." He was seeking to save His sanctuary.

In the Old Testament concept of cities of refuge, sanctuary referred to a place where a person guilty of a crime could flee to to save his life. Jesus took this concept and turned it upside down – saving us from destruction and cleansing us so that He could take sanctuary within us. He saves us to dwell in us to keep us safe from the effects of the world.

Now, when people talk about "sanctuary" in the context of buildings, they speak of something consecrated or set apart. But Jesus, by His Blood, has consecrated and sanctified forever:

> *And in accordance with this will [of God], we have been made holy (consecrated and sanctified) through the offering made once for all of the body of Jesus Christ (the Anointed One). (Hebrews 10:10 AMP)*

Jesus, being God in the flesh, could have chosen to dwell in the sanctuary of the temple built by Herod. He could have made that the seat of His earthly government. Instead, He prophesied the ruin of the physical temple and the erection of the spiritual temple. Throughout His time on earth, Jesus did most of His ministry in His surrounding communities. While he had been noted, on occasion, to teach in the synagogues, the only reference to Him being in the temple are the times when he cleansed it of the moneychangers.

Indeed, moving into the first-century Church of the book of Acts, we see the saints establishing local churches in people's homes. After Herod's temple, we do not see any structure in Scripture being built for the express purpose of worship or fellowship.

Jesus sought, found, and saved His sanctuary when He found and redeemed us from the clutches of sin and religion, bringing us into His kingdom so that His presence could abide with us forever!

We have been made his Temple! And wherever we go, the place of worship goes with us. Wherever we go, the presence of God goes, too!

The sanctuary is not a building! Our sanctuary is in Christ and His Sanctuary is in us!

Of course, it takes resources to build and maintain buildings. That said, what discussion of church would be complete without a discussion of its most controversial topic: Money.

Religion and Money

1 Timothy 6:10
For the love of money is the root of all
evil: which while some coveted after,
they have erred from the faith, and
pierced themselves through with many
sorrows.

THE SEED

How many of you have heard these?

I need 100 people to sow a $1000 seed...

This church is good ground to sow seed into...

Sow a $103 seed for your healing...

God says, "Sow seed and I'll bless you..."

There is an interesting characteristic about seed – it multiplies on its own! Whether it's seed for grain, seed for vegetables, or seed of people, the unique characteristic of seed is its ability to reproduce after its own kind.

Now, when the Bible talks about seed, it is either speaking of plant, animal, human, or the Word of God.

Never, ever, ever does the Bible refer to seed as money! You absolutely, positively, have to catch this! Do not be deceived – money is not "seed."

To take this into totality, all seed emanates from the Word of God:

> *And God said, Let the earth bring forth grass, the herb yielding seed, and the fruit tree yielding fruit after his kind, whose seed is in itself, upon the earth: and it was so. (Genesis 1:11)*

This corresponds to the Parable of the Sower, given by Jesus:

> *5 A sower went out to sow his seed: and as he sowed, some fell by the way side; and it was trodden down, and the fowls of the air devoured it. 6 And some fell upon a rock; and as soon as it was sprung up, it withered away, because it lacked moisture. 7 And some fell among thorns; and the thorns sprang up with it, and choked it. 8 And other fell on good ground, and sprang up, and bare fruit an hundredfold. And when he had said these things, he cried, He that hath ears to hear, let him hear. 9 And his disciples*

96

asked him, saying, What might this parable be? 10 And he said, Unto you it is given to know the mysteries of the kingdom of God: but to others in parables; that seeing they might not see, and hearing they might not understand. 11 Now the parable is this: The seed is the word of God. 12 Those by the way side are they that hear; then cometh the devil, and taketh away the word out of their hearts, lest they should believe and be saved. 13 They on the rock are they, which, when they hear, receive the word with joy; and these have no root, which for a while believe, and in time of temptation fall away. 14 And that which fell among thorns are they, which, when they have heard, go forth, and are choked with cares and riches and pleasures of this life, and bring no fruit to perfection. 15 But that on the good ground are they, which in an honest and good heart, having heard the word, keep it, and bring forth fruit with patience. (Luke 8:5-15)

Verse 11 is the Key Point of this Scripture – THE SEED IS THE WORD! The Word of God has the ability to reproduce after its own kind when sown into the hearts of men!

Let's take this line upon line, precept upon precept – this is corroborated by Galatians 3:16:

16 Now to Abraham and his seed were the promises made. He saith not, And to seeds, as of many; but as of one, And to thy seed, which is Christ.

Did you catch that? SEED – Paul is reiterating that Jesus is the seed because Jesus is The Word of God:

14 And the Word was made flesh, and dwelt among us, (and we beheld his glory, the glory as of the only begotten of the Father,) full of grace and truth. (John 1:14)

And we are offspring of God through Jesus, the firstborn:

15 Who is the image of the invisible God, the firstborn of every creature: 16 For by him were all things created, that are in heaven, and that are in earth, visible and invisible, whether they be thrones, or dominions, or principalities, or powers: all things were created by him, and for him: 17 And he is before all things, and by him all things consist. 18 And he is the head of the body, the church: who is the beginning, the firstborn from the dead; that in all things he might have the preeminence. 19 For it pleased the Father that in him should all fulness dwell; (Colossians 1:15-19)

Jesus said He is THE WAY, THE TRUTH, and THE LIFE (John 14:6). The chief characteristic of life is reproduction!

Here are a couple of scripture passages where a lot of Bible teachers get tripped up – the first:

> *10 Now he that ministereth seed to the sower both minister bread for your food, and multiply your seed sown, and increase the fruits of your righteousness; (2 Corinthians 9:10)*

This scripture is frequently touted to illustrate that you must take some seed to sow before you take seed from which to make bread. I submit to you that because Jesus is both the Word of God (the seed) and the Bread of Life (John 6:35), Paul is illustrating to us that Jesus is both our sustenance and our heritage.

And the second:

> *26 And he said, So is the kingdom of God, as if a man should cast seed into the ground; 27 And should sleep, and rise night and day, and the seed should spring and grow up, he knoweth not how. 28 For the earth bringeth forth fruit of herself; first the blade, then the ear, after that the full corn in the ear. 29 But when the fruit is brought forth, immediately he putteth in the sickle, because the harvest is come. (Mark 4:27-29)*

This passage of scripture is used to imply the process of sowing into a particular ministry. Actually, Jesus is illustrating the nature of life and that it is complex to the point it is not understood fully, and that there is a process to the seed sown.

I've gone through a process, here, of explaining seed. I'd like to take some time to fully uncouple seed from money.

There is nowhere in Scripture where seed equates with money. You know what money is? Money is a TOOL. Tools are used to bring about a result. You cannot put a plow in the ground and expect a harvest of plows. You can, however, use the plow to bust-up the ground to sow seed. And you can INVEST money to buy more or better plows. But if you try to put money in the ground, well, I'll let Scripture speak to this:

> *14 For the kingdom of heaven is as a man travelling into a far country, who called his own servants, and delivered unto them his goods. 15 And unto one he gave five talents, to another two, and to another one; to every man according to his several ability; and straightway took his journey. 16 Then he that had received the five talents went and traded with the same, and made them other five talents. 17 And likewise he that had received two, he also gained other two. 18 But he that had received one went and digged in the earth, and hid his lord's money. 19 After a long time the lord of those servants cometh, and reckoneth with them. 20 And so he that had received five talents came and brought other five talents, saying, Lord, thou deliveredst unto me five talents:*

behold, I have gained beside them five talents more. 21 His lord said unto him, Well done, thou good and faithful servant: thou hast been faithful over a few things, I will make thee ruler over many things: enter thou into the joy of thy lord. 22 He also that had received two talents came and said, Lord, thou deliveredst unto me two talents: behold, I have gained two other talents beside them. 23 His lord said unto him, Well done, good and faithful servant; thou hast been faithful over a few things, I will make thee ruler over many things: enter thou into the joy of thy lord. 24 Then he which had received the one talent came and said, Lord, I knew thee that thou art an hard man, reaping where thou hast not sown, and gathering where thou hast not strawed: 25 And I was afraid, and went and hid thy talent in the earth: lo, there thou hast that is thine. 26 His lord answered and said unto him, **Thou wicked and slothful servant, thou knewest that I reap where I sowed not, and gather where I have not strawed: 27 Thou oughtest therefore to have put my money to the exchangers, and then at my coming I should have received mine own with usury. 28 Take therefore the talent from him, and give it unto him which hath ten talents.** *29 For unto every one that hath shall be given, and he shall have abundance: but from him that hath not shall be taken away even that which he hath. 30 And cast ye the unprofitable servant into* *outer darkness: there shall be weeping and gnashing of teeth. (Matthew 25:14-30 — emphasis mine)*

Talents, as they are referred to here, are units of precious metal (usually gold or silver) of around 94 pounds (according to Easton's Bible Dictionary).

The salient point here is that the servant who buried his money (sowed it?) was on the business end of the wrath of his master. Follow the bold print. You cannot "sow" money because it has no ability to reproduce itself!

Money, at its best, is a tool that can be used to spread THE SEED, that is, the Word of God. Your time, talent, and treasure, cannot be sown. Money cannot reproduce after its own kind without lots of help! However, the Word of God is self-sustaining and self-reproducing, and we use tools such as money (buildings, television, internet, etc.) to help spread the seed. And whatever monetary resources we're blessed with we should give cheerfully with the sole expectation that your gift will be used for the express purpose of spreading the Gospel. Giving with a hope of getting something in return is not giving at all but investment!

I don't expect this teaching to endear me to many. However, it is my prayer that it serves to sharpen your discernment.

When you understand what the SEED really is, it will help you understand what tithing is...and isn't.

TITHING AND THE CHURCH

I am amazed at how tenaciously some folks cling to doctrine in spite of truth. In this book, I'm dealing with some very serious damage done to the church by the building of doctrine around situational Biblical text. I promise, you'll want to stick with me because you're going to hear some blockbuster truth that will shake your religious foundation to dust! That said, the one I want to deal with, here, is what may be everyone's favorite:

Tithing.

Now, I've dealt with this on multiple occasions in my blog and have empirically proven that tithing is not commanded for the New Testament believer. And before I get started down this path, let me say that I AM in favor of "grace giving," in other words, give because it is right, give cheerfully, give generously, and give consistently.

There is no Scripture to support tithing for the New Covenant saint. Period. In order to support this construct, you must both drag up and dust off a covenant that was buried with Jesus and stayed in the ground when He was resurrected or build an extra-biblical straw-man, like, "How do you expect the church to have operating capital?" To this, I respond, "If you require all that money to operate, you may need to re-evaluate the purpose of your local church body..."

Either way it doesn't work.

Proponents of tithing – by and large – go to Malachi chapter 3 to support their thesis. However, this falls flat when considering, a) Malachi was written to the priests, not the saints (Malachi 2:1), and b) That if Malachi is the template for the tithe, then the NT believer is beholden to the whole law – all 613 commandments (James 2:10). And a lot of NT believers – myself included – would be upset that we'd have to give up bacon to uphold the whole law!

Once the Malachi argument is laid to rest, tithing teachers turn to Abram (Abraham) and his encounter with Melchizedek. This is a comfortable place of retreat for the tithing crowd because they love to point out that this took place before the law. But we're going to flesh that duck out of that blind in just a moment.

Before we get to Melchizedek, we must firmly establish a fact about Abraham that tithing teachers conveniently omit here:

Abram was *rich*. He was rich when he left Ur of the Chaldees. And he was *RICHER* after his run-in with Pharaoh (Genesis 12:16, Genesis 13:2, 6). And, yet, there is no record of Abram tithing before or after encountering Melchizedek.

But back to the story…

Abram encounters Melchizedek, fat with the spoils of war. When he realized Melchizedek was the King of Salem (Peace), Abram broke bread with Melchizedek and gave him a tenth (tithe) of the spoils of war (Genesis 14:18-20). That's as good a basis for tithing but even that is untenable in the light of what Abram did next – he gave the rest (90 percent) to the King of Sodom so he would not be beholden to him. Yes, THAT Sodom! So what Abram did was give 10 percent to the Good King and 90 percent to the evil king. So, what we have is Abram basically hitting the lottery, giving 10 percent to the "church" and 90 percent to the world.

This alone should help you see the absurdity in this argument but, as they say, "wait, there's more…"

Deuteronomy 14 is a good indicator of what should be done with the tithe. First of all, let's do a quick level-set: The tithe was only applicable to agricultural occupations. It dealt with 10 percent of agricultural produce. Therefore, if you were a fisherman, a carpenter, a smith, or a physician, you did not tithe! This said, in Deuteronomy 14, the instruction is given that if the prospective tither lives too far from the temple, he can exchange the tithe for money, with which they can do the following:

> *And thou shalt bestow that money for whatsoever thy soul lusteth after, for oxen, or for sheep, or for wine, or for strong drink, or for whatsoever thy soul desireth: and thou shalt eat there before the Lord thy God, and thou shalt rejoice, thou, and thine household, (Deuteronomy 14:26)*

Did you catch that? Strong drink. That translates to beer, wine, or booze. Or "for whatsoever thy soul desireth." That is an unqualified statement!

In other words, spend your tithe money to get your party on! I'm not advocating alcohol consumption; I'm just pointing out what the Word says!

Also, the tithe only applied to agricultural production. It was not applicable to fishermen (like Peter), tentmakers (like Paul), coppersmiths, carpenters (like Jesus), etcetera!

Then, the supporters of tithing conveniently scurry to Matthew 23:23. For your reading convenience, I'll provide the text here:

> *Woe unto you, scribes and Pharisees, hypocrites! for ye pay tithe of mint and anise and cummin, and have omitted the weightier*

> *matters of the law, judgment, mercy, and*
> *faith: these ought ye to have done, and not*
> *to leave the other undone. (Matthew 23:23)*

Note three things here, 1) Jesus is talking to legalists who should know the law, 2) This statement took place when the law was in effect, and 3) Jesus did not command anyone to do this – he merely said they were following one part of the law while ignoring another!

Again, the tithing camp is left with a less-than-watertight argument.

Where I'd like to hang my hat, today, is on the last finger on the last rung of the teaching of the tithe until the whole thing falls into the abyss.

Hebrews 7.

There's far too much text here to cut-n-paste. The author of Hebrews dedicates a fair amount of text to tithing – or does he? Yes, the author speaks of tithing and Melchizedek but he also speaks about the superiority of the New Covenant versus the Old. This is a clear-cut example of taking a situational text and building doctrine around it. There is nothing here that commands the readers to observe and/or uphold the tithe.

The problem is context. The 7th chapter of Hebrews is in the midst of a stream of the author's thought that begins with the 5th chapter and ends with the 10th. In this passage of the text, the author meticulously juxtaposes the Old and

New Covenants, comparing them and contrasting them and driving home the point of the New Covenant being "more excellent."

Isolating chapter 7 to build a straw man for tithing is just bad theology.

The author of Hebrews is absolutely not building a case for tithing because, if he were, he would hinge this argument on the necessity of hanging on to parts of the Old Covenant. The salient question to be asked of every proponent of tithing is:

"Would you be better off under the law or are you better off under grace?" Or, "Are you better off under bondage or better off when set free?"

By the way, most Jews don't tithe – and they ARE still under the law!

Let me make one thing abundantly clear – I'm opposed to tithing but giving should be a hallmark of a true believer. Here's what Jesus had to say about giving:

> *Give, and it shall be given unto you; good measure, pressed down, and shaken together, and running over, shall men give into your bosom. For with the same measure that ye mete withal it shall be measured to you again. (Luke 6:38)*

And the Apostle Paul condensed it thusly:

But this I say, He which soweth sparingly shall reap also sparingly; and he which soweth bountifully shall reap also bountifully. Every man according as he purposeth in his heart, so let him give; not grudgingly, or of necessity:for God loveth a cheerful giver. (2 Corinthians 9:6-7)

You cannot live without loving and you can't love without giving! Give cheerfully. Give consistently. Give generously. That's grace giving!

Here's what the author of Hebrews is saying, in a nutshell:

Old is past – New is present
Old is bondage – New is liberty
Old was good – New is better

Do you get that? It's just that simple! You'd need to pay someone a heap of money to help you misunderstand this!

Don't give in to arm-twisting, extortionist tactics concerning giving. Giving that has to be coerced isn't giving, at all – it's robbery! And, while you're at it, don't buy into the fallacy that money is a seed.

Tithing is the gateway drug that introduces believers to all manner of church financial malarkey – like prophecy for profit.

PROPHETS AND PROFIT

There is nothing wrong with earning a profit. We all have the privilege of profiting from our labor. However, when it comes to laboring for the Kingdom of God, there are things we must do for which we should expect no return.

> *And when it was evening, his disciples came to him, saying, This is a desert place, and the time is now past; send the multitude away, that they may go into the villages, and buy themselves victuals. 16 But Jesus said unto them, They need not depart; give ye them to eat. 17 And they say unto him, We have here but five loaves, and two fishes. 18 He said, Bring them hither to me. 19 And he commanded the multitude to sit down on the*

grass, and took the five loaves, and the two
fishes, and looking up to heaven, he blessed,
and brake, and gave the loaves to his
disciples, and the disciples to the multitude.
20 And they did all eat, and were filled: and
they took up of the fragments that remained
twelve baskets full. 21 And they that had
eaten were about five thousand men, beside
women and children. (Matthew 14:15-21)

Now, in many churches, it's customary to sell fish dinners
and barbecue dinners to raise money for programs and
buildings, but this wasn't Jesus' model. Many folks,
today, would have sold the miraculous multiplication of
food to the folks on the hillside to pay the preacher, then
sold the twelve remaining baskets for the building fund!

Here's one that really gets me – folks who will sell
healing, deliverance, or the Word of God, itself for
money! How many preachers promise healing in
exchange for a "seed offering?" If Peter and John operated
as many modern preachers do, they'd have badgered the
lame man for a major offering upon his healing. Peter and
John exemplify what Jesus demonstrated to them
regarding healing; we should emulate this model.

And a certain man lame from his mother's
womb was carried, whom they laid daily at
the gate of the temple which is called
Beautiful, to ask alms of them that entered
into the temple; 3 Who seeing Peter and
John about to go into the temple asked an
alms. 4 And Peter, fastening his eyes upon
him with John, said, Look on us. 5 And he

111

gave heed unto them, expecting to receive something of them. 6 Then Peter said, Silver and gold have I none; but such as I have give I thee: In the name of Jesus Christ of Nazareth rise up and walk. 7 And he took him by the right hand, and lifted him up: and immediately his feet and ankle bones received strength. 8 And he leaping up stood, and walked, and entered with them into the temple, walking, and leaping, and praising God. 9 And all the people saw him walking and praising God: (Acts 3:2-9)

Far too many preachers seek to exploit the anointing of God for base gain. In the following passage of Scripture, below, "Simon the Sorcerer" sought to obtain the Power of God by the laying of hands so that he could manipulate people. Peter, through the power of the Holy Spirit, saw through Simon's ruse and rebuked him. It is shameful how many so-called "men and women of God" willingly prey on unsuspecting saints with promises of healing, deliverance, and prosperity in exchange for money. This is a practice that needs to cease, as it is in direct violation of Scripture.

And when Simon saw that through laying on of the apostles 'hands the Holy Ghost was given, he offered them money, 19 Saying, Give me also this power, that on whomsoever I lay hands, he may receive the Holy Ghost. 20 But Peter said unto him, Thy money perish with thee, because thou hast thought that the gift of God may be purchased with money. 21 Thou hast neither

part nor lot in this matter: for thy heart is
not right in the sight of God. (Acts 8:18-21)

Then, there are those who will use church as a venue for business. There are many folks who go to church to "network," passing out business cards and other marketing collateral, hoping to use God's people as a springboard to increased profits.

> *And Jesus went into the temple of God, and*
> *cast out all them that sold and bought in the*
> *temple, and overthrew the tables of the*
> *moneychangers, and the seats of them that*
> *sold doves, 13 And said unto them, It is*
> *written, My house shall be called the house*
> *of prayer; but ye have made it a den of*
> *thieves. 14 And the blind and the lame came*
> *to him in the temple; and he healed them.*
> *(Matthew 21:12-14)*

Here's where we miss the point of godly, Biblical prosperity – which is to use your blessing to be a blessing to others. In the first-century church, the Disciples of Christ sold their possessions and laid the proceeds at the feet of the Apostles, who in turn, distributed to everyone as they had need – AND NONE HAD LACK! Notice, here, that the people sold their possessions but the Apostles DID NOT make merchandise of their anointing! This is the miracle that happens when giving is done freely and cheerfully:

> *And the multitude of them that believed were*
> *of one heart and of one soul: neither said*
> *any of them that ought of the things which*

113

he possessed was his own; but they had all things common. 33 And with great power gave the apostles witness of the resurrection of the Lord Jesus: and great grace was upon them all. 34 Neither was there any among them that lacked: for as many as were possessors of lands or houses sold them, and brought the prices of the things that were sold, 35 And laid them down at the apostles 'feet: and distribution was made unto every man according as he had need. (Acts 4:32-35)

There is no one who will embrace this pattern of giving that will experience lack. The promise of blessing is not "pie-in-the-sky" in the "sweet-by-and-by," it is "ham-where-I-am" in the "sour-here-and-now!" Notice in the scripture, below, how Jesus assigns a hundred-fold blessing for those who will sacrifice all for the Gospel of the Kingdom:

Then Peter began to say unto him, Lo, we have left all, and have followed thee. 29 And Jesus answered and said, Verily I say unto you, There is no man that hath left house, or brethren, or sisters, or father, or mother, or wife, or children, or lands, for my sake, and the gospel's, 30 But he shall receive an hundredfold now in this time, houses, and brethren, and sisters, and mothers, and children, and lands, with persecutions; and in the world to come eternal life. 31 But many that are first shall be last; and the last first. (Mark 10:28-31)

114

One of my best friends has a business motto that resonates with me and provides a fitting close for this message: "Putting the Priority of People Over Profits." Search for purpose, not profit… find your purpose and profits of all types will follow.

It is the religious junk of profiteering prophets that steer many out of receiving the prosperity God desires for all His children.

PROSPERITY

The devil's power ends with the Kingdom of God and the earthly dominion of man, which Jesus came to restore. Because we are His emissaries in the earth, we are to be equipped with all sufficiency (spiritual and natural) to accomplish every good work (2 Corinthians 9:8), to have the expectation of material blessing (Mark 10:29-30), and to have abundant life (John 10:10). Prosperity not taught is just as bad as prosperity out of context. Biblical prosperity is part of the Kingdom Citizen's benefits package and MUST be taught in its proper context!

Let me ask you a question, dear reader. Do you have any children? If so don't you want the best for them? Isn't their prosperity and health a reflection of your ability and influence? If the answer is yes – and God is a better Father than you or I could ever be – surely God wants the best for us!

Religion has distorted Scripture to the point where prosperity is viewed as profane. In Mark, chapter 10, the Lord was not establishing a doctrine in telling the rich young ruler to sell all his possessions, he was speaking contextually to what the young man was yoked to; that is, his wealth. There is no instruction to take a vow of poverty or that wealth, in and of itself, is sinful.

Now, I'm not one of these pastors looking to fleece his flock; rather I'm blessed with a wonderful standard of living that is a blessing from God (I grew up poor – raised by a single mother with two siblings). And the Kingdom principles that God's Word has imparted to me, I share with others, and EVERY one who has applied them has seen an increase in their standard of living.

The Kingdom of God is not merely about "pie-in-the-sky-in-the-sweet-by-and-by;" rather, it's about wholeness, completion, nothing broken, nothing lacking!

Beside salvation, Kingdom provision includes deliverance, healing, and material blessing. Do you actually believe God wants you to live in lack in your earthly life? If so, then I'll pray fervently for you...and for all whom you teach!

Yes, we are not to look to the world for our supply or heap up treasure here, but we can have the earnest expectation of divine provision and earthly abundance that we may FLOW THROUGH to our brothers and sisters in need.

Now, if you decide to opt out on any Kingdom benefit, well, that is your decision. However I will RELENTLESSLY teach that God has abundance for you, NOW, not just in heaven.

Scripture is clear that poverty is not the will of God for the believer.

> *And Jesus answered and said, Verily I say unto you, There is no man that hath left house, or brethren, or sisters, or father, or mother, or wife, or children, or lands, for my sake, and the gospel's, 30 But he shall receive an hundredfold now in this time, houses, and brethren, and sisters, and mothers, and children, and lands, with persecutions; and in the world to come eternal life. (Mark 10:29-30)*

Here Jesus is saying if you LEAVE things for Him, you'll RECEIVE things from Him, IN THE HERE AND NOW, not just in the sweet-by-and-by!

But wait...there's more!

> *Foxes have holes and birds have nests, but the Son of Man has nowhere to lay his head (Luke 9:58).*

Folks who rail against what is commonly called the "prosperity gospel" frequently abuse this aforementioned scripture. We must consider the context of that statement. Jesus had nowhere to lay his head...in Samaria! The Samaritans would not receive Him because they felt slighted because Jesus had His face set toward Jerusalem:

> *And it came to pass, when the time was come that he should be received up, he stedfastly set his face to go to Jerusalem, And sent messengers before his face: and they went, and entered into a village of the Samaritans, to make ready for him. And they did not receive him, because his face was as though he would go to Jerusalem. (Luke 9:51-53).*

The above scripture is usually trotted out to make the case for a poor, homeless, vagabond Jesus. You can similarly make the case that Jesus, Himself, had a house...

> *Then Jesus turned, and saw them following, and saith unto them, What seek ye? They said unto him, Rabbi, (which is to say, being interpreted, Master,) where dwellest thou? 39 He saith unto them, Come and see. They came and saw where he dwelt, and abode with him that day: for it was about the tenth hour. (John 1:38-39)*

...One that he was proud of (Come and see – admittedly, this is an inference but you don't say "come and see" regarding another man's house)!

We're not done...

> *This he said, not that he cared for the poor; but because he was a thief, and had the bag, and bare what was put therein. (John 12:6)*

> *For some of them thought, because Judas had the bag, that Jesus had said unto him, Buy those things that we have need of against the feast; or, that he should give something to the poor. (John 13:29)*

Here are two references to a treasury (the bag). You don't need a treasury if you're a poor, itinerant minister!

Need more proof?

> *And a river went out of Eden to water the garden; and from thence it was parted, and became into four heads. 11 The name of the first is Pison: that is it which compasseth the whole land of Havilah, where there is gold; 12 And the gold of that land is good: there is bdellium and the onyx stone. (Genesis 2:10-12)*

Here God shows his intent to place material wealth at the hands of Adam!

120

We must dispense with the lie that poverty equals piety.

Here's the kicker...

> *And God is able to make all grace abound toward you; that ye, always having all sufficiency in all things, may abound to every good work: (2 Corinthians 9:8)*

Here Paul says ALL things. You CANNOT abound to anything in poverty! In order to represent the Kingdom and to do Kingdom work, we must be equipped with the means to do so!

Another refuge for the anti-prosperity religious crowd is the rich young ruler, whom Jesus was dealing with the fact he was yoked to his money (money was, in fact, his god), not earthly riches, themselves.

> *Then Jesus beholding him loved him, and said unto him, One thing thou lackest: go thy way, sell whatsoever thou hast, and give to the poor, and thou shalt have treasure in heaven: and come, take up the cross, and follow me. And he was sad at that saying, and went away grieved: for he had great possessions. And Jesus looked round about, and saith unto his disciples, How hardly shall they that have riches enter into the kingdom of God! And the disciples were astonished at his words. But Jesus*

answereth again, and saith unto them,
Children, how hard is it for them that trust
in riches to enter into the kingdom of
God! (Mark 10:21-24)

Jesus never commanded anyone to take a vow of poverty or expected anyone to give up anything without compensation. In fact, He promised that there would be abundance in store for those who sacrificed for the Gospel of the Kingdom – refer again to Mark 10:29-30

Now, does this mean every believer is called to be a millionaire or billionaire? No, that would be a perversion of scripture. However, it is abundantly clear that poverty does not equate with godliness and that it is the will of God for His children to prosper.

In summary...

Let them shout for joy, and be glad, that
favour my righteous cause: yea, let them say
continually, Let the Lord be magnified,
which hath pleasure in the prosperity of his
servant. (Psalms 35:27)

The Lord DELIGHTS (has pleasure in) the prosperity of His servant! You'd have to pay someone to misunderstand this!

Bottom line: Poverty IS NOT God's will for His children.

Religion and the World

John 17:16

They are not of the world, even as I am not of the world.

IS GOD IN CONTROL?

S adly, there are some that still believe that God is the author of calamity. The persistence of this belief results in some seriously schizophrenic Christianity. The truth is, God not only is not the author of sickness, pain, suffering, and calamity, and He does not control every minutia of human life.

If God simply controls everything, then there was no point in giving mankind dominion and free will. The Lord wishes that none perish, but that all come to repentance – yet hundreds of thousands die unsaved daily. If God simply controls everything, there is no point in doing anything. That reduces the Christian walk to a fatalistic, religious ritual. I think a lot of Scripture is abused for the purpose of perpetuating religious bondage.

What we need to do is look at the person of Jesus. He said if we see Him, we see the Father:

> *Jesus saith unto him, Have I been so long time with you, and yet hast thou not known me, Philip? he that hath seen me hath seen the Father; and how sayest thou then, Shew us the Father? (John 14:9).*

He said He only does what He sees the Father do:

> *Then answered Jesus and said unto them, Verily, verily, I say unto you, The Son can do nothing of himself, but what he seeth the Father do: for what things soever he doeth, these also doeth the Son likewise. (John 5:19).*

The author of Hebrews says Jesus is the express image of the Father:

> *Who being the brightness of his glory, and the express image of his person, and upholding all things by the word of his power, when he had by himself purged our sins, sat down on the right hand of the Majesty on high; (Hebrews 1:3).*

In this context, whom did Jesus make sick – or for that matter, allow to remain sick? None. Moreover, Jesus did not cause calamity; He calmed storms:

*And he arose, and rebuked the wind, and
said unto the sea, Peace, be still. And the
wind ceased, and there was a great
calm. (Mark 4:39).*

He healed the sick, cleansed lepers, raised the dead, and
preached Good News to the poor!

Indeed, when two of His disciples wanted to bring fire
from heaven on to folks who rejected Jesus, He rebuked
them:

*And when his disciples James and John saw
this, they said, Lord, wilt thou that we
command fire to come down from heaven,
and consume them, even as Elias did? But
he turned, and rebuked them, and said, Ye
know not what manner of spirit ye are
of. (Luke 9:54-55)*

Now, if God is causing these things (sickness, suffering,
and calamity) and Jesus is providing the cure, then Jesus
would be acting against the will of the Father, right?

Jesus said He came to do the Father's will (Luke 6:38).
And a house divided cannot stand (Matthew 12:25)!
Clearly Jesus' will was aligned with the Father's.

Jesus is the focal point of all Scripture. All Scripture
points to him and he is the living revelation of all
Scripture. In order to truly understand the nature and

character of God, we must center our studies on the Gospels.

It becomes clear that since Jesus did not bring about any of these things during His earthly ministry, and since the chastisement of our peace was upon Him, God isn't bringing about calamity, either.

You'd have to pay someone to help you misunderstand this!

So, if God isn't micromanaging everything, is he truly "sovereign?"

GOD AND SOVEREIGNTY

God is, indeed, sovereign. He created everything by His Word and He has the ability to influence and change any situation in the earth. Many theologians and their faithful followers operate under the presumption that nothing happens in the earth unless God either causes or permits or permits it.

In order to support this premise, some huge theological hurdles must be cleared.

To prove the incorrectness of the sovereignty premise, we must go – as it were – to the beginning. Let's take a look

128

at Genesis, chapter one (hereafter called, "God's Mission Statement"):

*And God said, Let us make man in our image, after our likeness: and **let them have dominion** over the fish of the sea, and over the fowl of the air, and over the cattle, and over all the earth, and over every creeping thing that creepeth upon the earth. So God created man in his own image, in the image of God created he him; male and female created he them. And God blessed them, and God said unto them, Be fruitful, and multiply, and replenish the earth, and subdue it: and **have dominion over** the fish of the sea, and over the fowl of the air, and over every living thing that moveth upon the earth. (Genesis 1:26-28, emphasis mine)*

Before we go any further, we need to establish literal definitions for both sovereign and dominion.

Sovereign (Source: Merriam-Webster):
Noun:
1. *one possessing or held to possess supreme political power or sovereignty*
2. *one that exercises supreme authority within a limited sphere*
3. *an acknowledged leader: arbiter*

.

Adjective:
1. *having unlimited power or authority*
2. *not limited*
3. *having independent authority and the right to govern itself*

.

Dominion (Source: Merriam-Webster)[:

Noun:

1. *the power to rule*
2. *control of a country, region, etc.*
3. *the land that a ruler or government controls*

Next, we need to level-set and establish a working definition for both sovereign and dominion.

Based on the definition of Sovereign, and our Scriptural understanding of God, we can safely conclude that God is, indeed, a Monarch with supreme authority, who is independent, royal, of the highest magnitude, preeminent in all things, greatest in degree, and above all things.

Based on the definition of Dominion, and our Scriptural understanding of Man in relation to God that he has been given authority in the earth, which is a territory or colony of Heaven, and is self-governing but owing tribute to the King of kings.

In neither natural nor any scriptural definition is it ever said that God simply controls everything!

That's a tough one to swallow, especially for the "God is in control" crowd. Yes, God created everything. Yes, everything depends upon God for its life or being. But, no, God does not control everything. God is not responsible for natural disasters or the deaths of children. To ascribe these things to God would make him equivalent to an abusive parent.

Free will is essential to God's relationship with man. If there were no free will there would be neither need for dominion nor would He have allowed Adam to transgress against Him. It is God's will that all are saved (2 Peter 3:9), but are they? It is God's will that all are prosperous and in health (3 John 2), but are they? They aren't – and it's because God's children frequently do not exercise their dominion franchise to change those things!

This sovereignty is essential to two of the far ends of the Christian spectrum: At one end lie the doctrine of election – that some are born into salvation, while others are born to go to hell. At the other end lies the belief that Jesus' sacrifice on the cross means that all are going to heaven and none are going to hell.

Both are incorrect because neither accounts for the will of man. God through His Holy Spirit is a gentleman; He never forces His will on anyone. A person may be presented with the Good News of Jesus and resists it as a matter of prerogative. And even though God provided for salvation for the whole world – and He could, by creative right – He doesn't force it upon everyone.

In fact, God wants us to take authority over situations and circumstances in the earth. Jesus presented us with a paradigm for this:

> *And Jesus answering saith unto them, Have faith in God. For verily I say unto you, That whosoever shall say unto this mountain, Be thou removed, and be thou cast into the sea; and shall not doubt in his heart, but shall*

131

believe that those things which he saith shall come to pass; he shall have whatsoever he saith. Therefore I say unto you, What things soever ye desire, when ye pray, believe that ye receive them, and ye shall have them. (Mark 11:22-24)

Without going too deep, the original text in Mark 11:22, "...have faith in God," actually reads more like, "have the God kind of faith." In other words, have the faith that gives you boldness to exercise dominion. That dominion is actually delegated authority — it is power given to us from the time of creation!

Understanding God's sovereignty is essential in exercising our role as stewards of the earth and regents of His authority. And this understanding ultimately determines whether we will sheepishly look to the sky for Jesus' return or look outward with determination to take territory for the Kingdom of God.

RELIGION AND THE RAPTURE

T he event we commonly call "The Rapture" will happen only when The Gospel of the Kingdom is preached fully throughout the nations (Matthew 24:14). The full Gospel has neither been preached in its entirety, nor is it fully preached throughout the world. We need to be diligent about renewing our minds, busying our hands, and mobilizing our feet...We have a lot of work to do!

In Ephesians 5:27, The Apostle Paul writes Jesus is coming for a church without spot (backbiting, gossip, leadership failure), wrinkle (denominations, musical disagreements, day-of-worship), or blemish (racism, cultural divides). In other words, we have a lot of washing and ironing to do before the wedding!

133

Why are we looking for the way out? Jesus came to restore the DOMINION originally given by God (Genesis 1:26-28) and lost by man. He gave us durable power of attorney (John 14:13-14, John 15:16, John 16:23-24,26) to be AGENTS of His AUTHORITY in the earth. Instead of looking to leave (fear-based) we need to be invading and influencing the earth with God's will, culture, and intent (faith-based) -- in other words, WE NEED A TAKEOVER MENTALITY!

If you're saved and all you're doing is trying to discern the signs of the Lord's return, you're not fulfilling the Great Commission (Matthew 28:19-20). Get off your Blessed Assurance and go forth INTO THE WORLD, winning souls AND making disciples in the name of Jesus!

Frankly, I'm tired of hearing preaching and teaching on the exit strategy when Jesus clearly laid out a takeover strategy!

It is a correct assessment that we should be "rapture-ready." However, just like there is an overabundance of pastors/preachers that are teaching holiness as readiness, there is equally a lack of those who are equipping saints to rule and reign where they are.

There is an old saying that B-I-B-L-E means *BASIC INSTRUCTIONS BEFORE LEAVING EARTH*. The Holy Spirit gave me a variation on this: ***BASIC INSTRUCTIONS BEFORE LIVING ETERNALLY***!

This is important because many people are taught that Jesus came, died, and was raised simply to punch our ticket to heaven. The truth is, we should be preparing to take territory for the Kingdom of God, not look for the exits!

Eternal life begins with the new birth. Eternal life is abundant, victorious life. It's not about going to heaven but bringing heaven to earth.

Religion teaches folks how to prepare to leave (pie-in-the-sky in the sweet-by-and-by) but relationship with God through Jesus equips saints how to live victorious lives in this realm (some-ham-where-I-am in the sour-here-and-now)!

The reality is that if God is just (and we can all agree He is) and that is all there is to it, when we accept Jesus as Lord and Savior, a la Romans 10:9-10, we would be raptured out on the spot.

But that doesn't happen, right? That's because it is our responsibility to bring as many as we can to Christ-consciousness, because it is God's desire that none perish, but all come to repentance (2 Peter 3:9). And while we remain, we have the promise of abundant life (John 10:10) with benefits (Psalm 103:2). We also have a promise of a life NOT free from tribulation, rather, overcoming the tribulation in Christ!

Also, for all the married brothers reading this, go back to your wedding day...did you have any involvement in your bride being ready for the marriage ceremony? Chances are, no! But your expectation is that she would come down the aisle clean, and orderly: makeup tight, nails done, hair fierce! You would likely have thought twice if she came down said aisle dirty and disheveled. Yet, today, that's what we have. Racism, denominational dissent, doctrinal disagreement, musical mayhem, etc., are spots, wrinkles, and blemishes!

The Church, today, is a bride-to-be coming off a three-day crack binge. Do we really think Jesus is coming for such a disheveled mess?

Nope!

That's where the dominion authority — the durable power of attorney of the name of Jesus — comes in! We need to be about the necessary washing (with the water of the Word, Ephesians 5:26) and ironing (Proverbs 27:17) so we may be found ready when our bridegroom comes!

That's why the five-fold ministry of Ephesians 4 needs to be about the work of equipping the saints with the understanding of salvation, knowledge of holiness, revelation of righteousness, and the doctrine of dominion! Instead of this, we have, at one extreme, those who would hobble the saints with religious junk (yep, I said it) and, at the other, those who abandon the true Gospel for motivational speaking.

We are to rule and reign with Jesus (Revelation 5:10) forever. This life is more than just the dress rehearsal; it is the opening act for your eternal destination!

I know this is deep! It is my sincere prayer that deep will continue to call out to deep, and that the Body of Christ will turn its face from the slipshod to the sincere!

Now that we understand that it is our responsibility to subdue the earth, we will need to understand that this doesn't mean subduing people.

RELIGION, RACE, AND CULTURE

B efore I get too far down the road in this chapter, I want to say that I will not discuss the specifics of racism. This is a touchy subject and can easily get in the weeds. Race and culture, together, comprise the proverbial "third rail" of civilized society.

That said, I firmly believe that racial harmony is only found in the full revelation of God's unconditional Love and Grace.

I will, however dedicate a bit of ink to the subject of prejudice and bigotry concerning race and culture in the

138

Body of Christ. It's been said that ignorance is the mother of prejudice and bigotry. If this is true, their likely father is religion.

From Christianity in the Crusades to the advent of ISIS, division and, often, decimation stem from viewing individuals and groups through the lens of our religious sensibilities.

A little working definition is in order. Prejudice is when you have issues with an individual or group without having much information about them, whereas bigotry is when you have sufficient information to dispel any prejudice but choose to dislike them, anyway.

The church has done a great job in perpetuating racial strife. From the crusades, which sought to purge the influence of Islam from the holy land, to the inquisitions, which targeted Moors in Europe, to the colonization of the undeveloped world, to the complicity of the Church in the proliferation of slavery, to its role in the Holocaust, the church has had a hand in many of the racial and cultural issues facing the world.

This is, however, the church at its worst. This is what happens when the church is governed by religion. It is the rules and regulations of religion that separates people. The church, when under the influence of religion becomes an agent of control. And one of the easiest ways to control people is to pit them against one another.

On the other hand, the church has also been instrumental in the abolition of slavery and the civil rights movement. Key leaders in the church saved many Jewish lives during the reign of the Nazis. And the Orthodox Church kept Christianity alive in the Soviet Union.

The Body of Christ is the most ethnically diverse group on earth. We are at our best when we are unified around the truth of Jesus Christ, not when we are divided along the lines of race, language, or culture.

There is no force that is more uniting than the Gospel. Because God's Love and Grace are unconditional, it makes the cross the most level playing field on the planet. Here's what Paul had to say about it:

> *28 There is neither Jew nor Greek, there is neither bond nor free, there is neither male nor female: for ye are all one in Christ Jesus. 29 And if ye be Christ's, then are ye Abraham's seed, and heirs according to the promise. (Galatians 3:28-29 KJV)*

If we were to fully embrace the words Paul penned here to the church at Galatia, there would be no prejudice, bigotry, or racism. Cultural and language barriers would fall. Everyone in the Body of Christ would put aside preconceived notions about people based on their ethnicities or places of origin. Disciples of Christ would cease to see one another as components in a religious mechanism but as organisms within a collective, organic body.

Just like man separated himself from God through sin, the church has had a hand in the separation of people along racial and cultural lines. And just like God sent a man in the person of Jesus Christ to fix the problem of sin, the church will need us to step up to remedy the world's racial and cultural ills.

IS THERE REALLY DEVIL'S MUSIC?

There are a many folks who, sadly, lament the use of "unacceptable" genres of music in church. These same folks call music outside the scope of traditional hymns, "devil's music," and point an accusing finger at churches that eschew traditional music, saying they are being influenced by the world.

Let's take a look at this.

The Bible tells us that satan was once the equivalent of the minister of music in Heaven. Here's how the Word described him:

Thou hast been in Eden the garden of God;
every precious stone was thy covering, the
sardius, topaz, and the diamond, the beryl,
the onyx, and the jasper, the sapphire, the
emerald, and the carbuncle, and gold: the
workmanship of thy tabrets and of thy pipes
was prepared in thee in the day that thou
wast created. (Ezekiel 28:13)

Tabrets and pipes, here, refer to musical instruments. In other words, Lucifer – before the fall – was a jewel-covered, walking, talking, musical instrument; one that was created by God. I submit to you, dear reader, God created music and, therefore, all music belongs to Him.

The devil is a spiritual eunuch – he is sterile and impotent. He cannot create anything – all the devil can do is pervert and distort that which is already created. Just like he perverted and distorted the serpent to deceive mankind, he also perverts and distorts music to the same end.

So how does the devil pervert and distort music? By influencing lyricists to write words that do not glorify God. There is no such thing as "the devil's music" because satan cannot create anything; he can only pervert and distort. Why? Because every note, rest, bar, measure, and scale belong to God.

I believe the flow of music is bi-directional. Isaac Watts wrote many of his beloved hymns to pub music, which was the scandalous music of the day. The sound of Motown was influenced by Gospel music and the Blues influenced Southern Gospel. Historically, there has been an ebb-and-flow of music from spiritual-to-secular-and back.

Some of the greatest secular artists have begun as Gospel singers and musicians. Likewise, there are a number of secular artists who have abandoned worldly music for the Gospel.

We, as the Body of Christ, need to stop demonizing artists and musicians. If the music you hear doesn't appeal to you, feel free to exercise your right to not listen.

That said, bring on hip-hop, grunge, and dust-country if the net effect is winning souls!

LEADING OR LORDING

I once posted this question on Facebook, "PASTORS: Are you hoarding and lording or leading and feeding?" and received precious few responses. I was actually surprised because I thought most would stand up and claim that they were doing the latter and not the former. I have come to the conclusion that far too many pastors and leaders are controversy-averse, shying away from anything that moves us out of our comfort zones. We need to stop this and start facing difficult subject matter head-on.

Picture this scenario: one Sunday a month, instead of packing the pews, listening to the latest solo and the whoop of the man of God, how about we deploy into our respective communities and manifest the kingdom. Imagine the impact if you go to someone's door and ask him or her, "What can I do for you, today?" Some folks don't need a material blessing; rather, they just need a person to talk to, or someone to speak a life-changing word to their children. But for those who do need a material blessing, let's take the money that has been set aside for bigger, grander facilities and use it to really bless someone! You know, food, clothing, and gas money!

We need to be preaching the Love of God and the Liberty in Christ. We need to preach the Grace of God, which is God's unmerited favor and unlimited power, not whether a woman wears pants or whether a man has long hair! We need to teach the blessing of giving, minus the bondage. You know what I'm talking about: telling folks that if they don't tithe, God will get the money from them in medical bills or something else. As if God, who created EVERYTHING with HIS WORD, actually needs our money!

We are called to be separate – a peculiar people (I Peter 2:9). Trouble is, nobody wants to be peculiar. Folks want to be normal, living in their insular, climate-controlled homes, working their ordinary 9-5 jobs, and worshipping in their big, pretty churches. Peculiar means UNUSUAL or DIFFERENT; we are called to stand out, not blend in! Being peculiar is mobilizing God's unconditional Love and Grace to a world that is persuaded that religion has judged it and found it evil. We need to get out of our collective comfort zones and get out and minister the medicine of Jesus Christ to the world. Are we going to be content with increasing our membership rolls or are we going out to make disciples?

Discipleship is often viewed as being hard because at its core is discipline. While it does takes discipline to be physically, fiscally, and spiritually fit, discipleship must also be practiced in love and be nurturing in its application. Discipleship should be a prelude to heaven – that is, it should be enjoyable, educational, and edifying.

We need to be about the work laid out in Ephesians 4:11-16, training and equipping the saints to get out and do the work of the Kingdom, not just fill a space in a pew.

Now, if you are a pastor or leader reading this and you can look yourself in the mirror and know this doesn't apply to you, please let it roll off your back. On the other hand, if you are convicted by these words, say "ouch," repent (change your mind for the better), roll up your sleeves and get to work!

God loves you and so do I. Let's get the work of the Kingdom done!

LEADERSHIP

The hallmark of a great leader is that they not only leave organizations in BETTER shape than when they arrived but also they leave the PEOPLE around them in better shape!

Good leaders equip and edify; poor leaders rob and tear down (John 10:10).

Having been a leader in both corporate America and in ministry, I submit the following:

Corporate America was at its zenith between 1935 and 1985. It was eminently successful because captains of industry were tested in the battlefields of WW1, WW2, Korea, and Vietnam. These folks understood the difference between leadership and management. Today, we have precious few corporations and institutions that have any combat-tested leaders among their ranks; just a bunch of B-school grads that fawn and swoon over numbers with no regard for human capital.

Likewise, in ministry, we are seeing the advent of pulpit managers instead of preaching leaders. In ministry, we're seeing increased attention to monetary and material management without the manifestation of the power of God or the development and discipling of men. This is not an indictment of all ministerial leaders but it is an eerily growing trend.

I think corporate America would benefit from conscripted military service; indeed, there would be a fallout-benefit to the country at large. Likewise, the church needs to start reaching out to young people, engaging them in stewardship and service; thus equipping them to be leaders. Kingdom leadership begins with service and continues with stewardship.

In both cases, the leadership paradigm should be based on Jesus, who led and taught by example and, ultimately, laid down His life for those in His charge.

That's my $.02...

The true cost of leadership (and their corresponding titles) can be counted on four points:

1. *Time*: a true leader avails him or herself of their most valuable resource. If you do not have time to pour into those who look to you for leadership, you are not a true

leader. You must have time to counsel and to be counseled. Your time must be sown of love; if you're just marking time, you're wasting time. I've told many that the only thing more valuable to me than my time is your time.

2. *Talent*: you must be giving of your talent in a loving and generous manner. Whatever your gift is, you MUST make it available to those in your care or sphere-of-influence. If you're hoarding your talent or charging exorbitant fees or honorariums for manifesting it, you're out of order.

3. *Treasure*: most church leadership has this backward – they look for spiritual sons and daughters to support them financially. Last time I checked, parents typically support their children until they are capable of supporting themselves. Many pastors fully expect their members to support them but will turn a deaf ear and a blind eye to a member in need. That is COMPLETELY out of order! My Bible says God loves a cheerful giver – and I'm willing to wager that He REALLY loves generous, cheerful giving on the part of leadership.

4. *Truth*: the biggest cost of leadership, and the one most ignored, is the sowing of the Truth – that is, God's Word. Only God's Word, not your time, talent, or treasure, can bring lasting change to every situation to which it is applied. We must be generous with the Word, especially the Gospel of Jesus Christ (The Gospel of the Kingdom) as to the sinner, it is the Good News of salvation; to the sick, it is the Good News of healing; to the tormented and oppressed, it is the Good News of deliverance; and, to the poor, it is the Good News of prosperity.

Your comfort zone is a dangerous place. Nothing moves without agitation! True, the good leader doesn't FORCE you out; rather he equips you to manage the transition out of your comfort zone. There is no growth without stretching.

The Bible says no man embarks upon building something without counting up the cost. Likewise, no person should embrace the mantel of leadership without calculating the cost. It is this lack of introspection and godly assessment that has caused the dearth of true leadership in the Church today.

It will take cultivation of leaders to advance the Kingdom Jesus built.

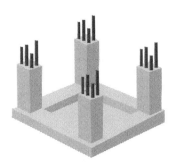

ADVANCING THE KINGDOM

Far too many folks have no concept of what advancing the Kingdom of God means because they have no concept of Kingdom. Too many folks are so caught up in religious rigmarole that they completely miss the revelation of relationship.

The Kingdom of God IS NOT religion, it is the Government of God (Isaiah 9:6-7) – yet many reduce what should be a relationship between a loving, powerful, Father and his earthly offspring to a weak, vain, religious experience. Jesus said, "upon this rock (truth) I will build my church (ekklesia or Government) and the gates of hell will not prevail against it" (Matthew 16:18).

Jesus wasn't talking about a social club for the saints, either. Yet, that's what the modern church is largely reduced to.

Our relationship with God must manifest itself in the expressed power that raised Jesus from the dead through us – the children of God. Yet many refuse to accept those things that Jesus died for BESIDES the salvation of the soul, namely deliverance from demonic oppression and bodily healing.

Many of us understand what it is to be a United States citizen. If you've ever traveled abroad, your citizenship has traditionally meant that foreign governments could not abuse or mistreat you, lest the force of the US government would fall upon them. But we lack understanding of what it means to be a Kingdom citizen – that the very *dunamis* (the Greek word where "dynamite" comes from) power of God is what empowers us!

And this lack of understanding of Royal Government clouds the understanding of men to the point they seek to build their own little fiefdoms instead of the Kingdom Jesus said it is the Father's good pleasure to give us (Luke 12:32). The purpose of ANY earthly ministry is to equip the saints until we all come together in unity of the faith (Ephesians 4:11-13). That means we should be equipping to SEND, not aiming to HOARD.

Where purpose is unknown, abuse is inevitable! The reason there is so much bickering and dissension among Christians is that too many want to esteem their opinions above the Word of God. The net of this has yielded a powerless Christianity that is unattractive to the world. Instead of being ambassadors for Christ, many of us have become representatives of vain religion and, because of this, we are seen as indistinguishable from the world's other religions.

To those in ministry and church leadership, I say, "stay in your lane; run your race!" Anything that bears the signature of God will be mocked by the world and will be lusted after by vain religion but, at the end of the day, will be eminently successful. Continue to equip, encourage, and edify the saints, demonstrating BY EXAMPLE what leadership born of love looks like!

HELL

Of all Christian doctrines, few have more holes in it than the doctrine of hell. Before I get started here, let me say that while my beliefs on hell are evolving, I believe that hell is real and it is represents real, eternal separation from God. I also believe that it is the final destination of satan, his demons, and those who reject Jesus.

That said, it is important to understand what hell is not. For starters, hell is not the devil's base of operations. It is not the place demons go hang out when they aren't afflicting people on earth. Contrary to some folks who reject Jesus, it is not a "party place."

One of the things that never ceased to amaze me is when folks say, "no devil in hell can stop me," or "no devil in hell can hold me back."

The truth of the matter is that no demon or devil that is sent to hell can torment anyone. Why? Because once they are in hell, there is no coming back. hell is a prison created for the devil and his minions, and we know that Jesus defeated satan at the cross and embarrassed him (Colossians 2:15). Therefore, we can conclude that with the devil convicted and sentenced, he is an escaped fugitive.

More to the point, hell was never created as a place of torment for mankind. Here is what Jesus said hell is created for:

> Then shall he say also unto them on the left hand, Depart from me, ye cursed, into everlasting fire, prepared for the devil and his angels: (Matthew 25:41)

Did you catch that? hell was created as a prison for the devil and demons.

Now, here's the deal, condemnation is the prescription for only those who deny Jesus:

> He that believeth on him is not condemned: but he that believeth not is condemned already, because he hath not believed in the name of the only begotten Son of God. (John 3:18)

So, anyone who does not believe on Jesus is already condemned. These folks are destined for eternal separation from God – which is the literal definition of death.

Glory to God, though, there is a solution:

> *For whosoever shall call upon the name of the Lord shall be saved. (Romans 10:13)*

That's good news – all who believe enough to call upon the name of Jesus will be saved. Going back to John 3:18, everyone who believes on Jesus is not condemned.

Another troubling aspect about how hell is presented to the non-believer is that the whole concept of "hell or the highway" or "turn or burn" is not what Jesus taught at all. Jesus never tried to scare anyone into entering into the Kingdom of God. Rather, He strove to love everyone into the Kingdom. Jesus told everyone to repent (which means "have a change of mind," not "confess your sins) but he never threatened anyone with hell.

Which brings up an interesting question: Why are so many preachers hell-bent on preaching hell? After all, hell is not good news, no matter how you slice it. Jesus commissioned all believers to preach the Gospel – that is, Good News. One of the unfortunate consequences of hellfire and brimstone preaching is that instead of lifting up Jesus to draw all men unto Him, this kind of preaching sends more people heading for the hills than bringing them to Christ.

I believe the root of this lies in that it is easier to control people through fear than it is when you give them liberty. There is great Grace in the preaching of the Gospel but Grace is absent in preaching hell.

The bottom line is this: there is no one whose fate is predetermined to go to hell. Likewise, Jesus died to make heaven available to all but all who choose to receive it.

What this means is that hell is not a looming reality for those who are in Christ:

> *There is therefore now no condemnation to them which are in Christ Jesus, who walk not after the flesh, but after the Spirit. (Romans 8:1)*

If you are saved – that is, Christ-conscious – you are in Christ…NOW! And because you are IN Christ, you no longer walk after the flesh!

And the better news is that the detour from eternal separation from God is to simply call on the name of Jesus!

OUT OF THE FIRE

 One of the most important things we do as Kingdom Citizens is win souls. Every soul won for Jesus is one soul that will not spend eternity in eternal separation from God. The important – and I mean, IMPORTANT – thing is that we are set on making disciples, not mere converts.

One of the things you'll hear about the importance of soul winning is that you save souls from hell. And the conventional wisdom is that when you save a soul from separation from God, you pull them out of the fire.

And if this is your assumption, you're partially right. Let's take a look at a key passage of Scripture:

> *22 And have mercy on those who doubt; 23 save others by snatching them out of the*

fire; to others show mercy with fear, hating even the garment stained by the flesh. (Jude 1:22-23 ESV)

The first thing we need to know, here, is that we must have compassion. We must have a heart of compassion. Jesus said by our love shall all men know we are His disciples (John 13:24-25). So, then, love is the hallmark of salvation. If we reverse-engineer this, we see that compassion is a chief component of love because Jesus had compassion for all who came to Him. If we back this up a step more, we find that empathy is key to compassion.

When Mark writes that Jesus loved the rich young ruler (Mark 10:21), it means He looked into his heart to find what he was yoked to (seeing things through his eyes) before telling him what he needed to do to inherit eternal life.

I say all that to say, if we have no compassion, no empathy, it's likely that love is absent. And if love is missing, salvation is suspect.

So, here Jude is saying that we must have mercy (compassion) on those who doubt. Here, we're looking not only at non-believers but those who have unbelief. In Mark, chapter 9 we see the account of the boy with a demon that caused seizures. When the disciples couldn't heal him, Jesus came and told them that all things are possible to he who believes (v.23). The father then replied, "I believe; help my unbelief." The mature believer believes without doubt – however, the mature believer also does not chide the immature believer for a lack of faith or belief.

Far too frequently – often by well-meaning saints – believers are criticized for lack of results. You suffered a financial calamity? You must lack faith. You didn't get healed? You must be in unbelief. You experienced a death in the family? Must be some hidden sin…

You get the idea. And, thinking they're ministering "tough love," they wind up shipwrecking the faith of someone. The landscape of life is littered with people with whom the love of God had been shared, only to be subsequently hit in the head by religion.

Religion takes no prisoners. At the very best, it's fear-tactics produce converts but will never produce disciples!

Now we get to the meaty-middle of the message – pulling folks from the fire (v.23)…

When firefighters rescue someone from a burning building, they go into the building to get them. Never have you heard a firefighter tell anyone, "…if you just come to the fire station, we can save you." Nope! Like the firefighter, we need to leave the four walls of church and go get folks. And, again like the firefighter, we don't have to tell folks the building is burning.

They know.

Now – hear me on this, because this is a theological game-changer – the fire we pull folks out of ain't hell. Hell is a final destination and you can't do anything for anyone there. You can, however, pull folks out of a burning vehicle that's headed to destruction! Peter spoke of this:

> *Beloved, do not be surprised at the fiery trial when it comes upon you to test you, as though something strange were happening to you. (1 Peter 4:12 ESV)*

That's what we're pulling folks out of – the fiery trials of life. And you don't have to harp on the danger of the fire; you need to tell them about how to get to safety.

And, by the way, if God is the one who brings someone to – or puts them into – the fiery trial, then we're out of order for trying to pull them out!

There is a theological – and, dare I say, religious – mindset that says you have to "balance Grace with truth." This school-of-thought supposes that you have to balance Grace and Love with "the fear of the Lord." Well, let me tell you Grace and Love are the truth of God and they are personified in Jesus!

The fear spoken of here is the reverence of God. I cannot say it enough; God is not the architect or the broker of fear – that's what the devil does. 2 Timothy 1:7 says God didn't give us the spirit of fear. That brings us to the killing of a sacred cow:

If God didn't give the saints a spirit of fear, why do many saints insist on using the spirit of fear to win souls?

The best way to win souls is to tell them about the too-good-to-be-true-news of God's unconditional Love and Grace, not fear of punishment! There's plenty of fear in the world and many thoughts and actions not under the captivity of Christ will heighten these fears. Perfect love casts out fear:

> There is no fear in love, but perfect love casts out fear. For **fear has to do with punishment**, and whoever fears has not been perfected in love (emphasis mine). (1 John 4:18 ESV)

And fear has to do with punishment. So, when you start preaching hellfire to folks, you're preaching fear and not faith.

And when we pull folks out, the garment we are supposed to hate is the effects of sin and the works of the flesh. In other words, we hate the garment but not the wearer. It's that whole judgment thing – we judge people by their appearances and, sometimes, folks are clothed in the effects of their sins and trials. But when we are in judgment mode, we tend to lack empathy and, when we lack empathy, we fail to minister in love.

Here's the bottom line – when we share Jesus with folks, it should never be with fear. We should be fearless in sharing and always sharing Love. You don't have to tell folks they're wrong – most of them already know it. What you need to share with them is THE BETTER WAY!

You know, The Way, The Truth, and The Life!

Religion and You

John 17:20
Neither pray I for these alone, but for
them also which shall believe on me
through their word;

WORD POWER

Y our words have power! God created everything with words. Then He created us in His image and likeness to look and act like Him. God created us to be a "speaking spirit" like Himself. He gave us words to create in the earth realm as He did in the heavenly realm.

Here's an account where Jesus illustrated the power of our words...

> *And Jesus answered them, Have faith in God. 23 Truly, I say to you, whoever says to this mountain, Be taken up and thrown into the sea, and does not doubt in his heart, but believes that what he says will come to pass,*

it will be done for him. 24 Therefore I tell
you, whatever you ask in prayer, believe that
you have received it, and it will be yours.
(Mark 11:22-25)

So, if we believe and not doubt – standing in faith that we already have what we've asked for – we have the assurance that the answer to our request will be yes and amen!

But here's the deal: once you're born-again, you're spirit is perfected once and forever. You will *never* be any better, spiritually, than when you first accept Jesus as Lord and Savior. However, we must renew our mind to align with our spiritual reality (Romans 12:2). This is both essential and critical because, as your mind goes, so goes your body.

Thou art snared with the words of thy
mouth, thou art taken with the words of thy
mouth. (Proverbs 6:2)

The origins of a thought...

When a thought occurs, we need to bring it into captivity and to the obedience of Jesus Christ:

3 For though we walk in the flesh, we do not
war after the flesh: 4 (For the weapons of
our warfare are not carnal, but mighty
through God to the pulling down of strong
holds;) 5 Casting down imaginations, and

166

every high thing that exalteth itself against
the knowledge of God, and bringing into
captivity every thought to the obedience of
Christ; (2 Corinthians 10:3 –5)

That means EVERY thought – good and bad! This will help discipline your thought life by keeping your mind aligned with your born-again spirit. Align every thought that crops up in your mind with the Word of God!

We also need to test the spirit behind the thought to see if it was from God:

Beloved, do not believe every spirit, but test
the spirits to see whether they are from God,
for many false prophets have gone out into
the world. (1 John 4:1)

This is why your prayer life is essential to a successful Christian walk. When you take time to align every thought with the Word of God and submit your thoughts to God in prayer, you learn to discern between good thoughts and evil ones!

Not every thought is from God! The notion to sin in the Garden of Eden was a thought planted by satan. When Nimrod set out to build the tower of Babel, that certainly wasn't a thought from God. When Abraham and Sarah set out to accelerate God's promise, that wasn't a thought from God. And when Judas thought to betray Jesus that was not a God thought.

167

Here's a litmus test for your thoughts: if the thought lacks creative power and/or compassion, it ain't from God! Remember, satan cannot create anything; he can only pervert and distort!

One more thing, God knows your heart and mind...the devil only knows what you tell him. In the Garden, the devil did not know which tree Adam and Eve could not eat from; he had to con the information out of Eve!

Everything begins with a thought...

One thing we need to clearly understand is that EVERYTHING in the natural begins in the spiritual. Here's an example: before a building is built, it is first conceived in the mind. Once conceived in the mind, it is ushered into the natural with a spoken word. Once the word is given, plans are executed and resources are brought to bear to bring the building into existence.

Every thought is a brick in a potential stronghold. You have to take a thought captive before it takes you captive! To take one brick captive is not a mean feat; to bring down a stronghold definitely is!

Every thought that you speak, you take ownership of. For example, if you confess sickness over yourself, you're claiming that sickness as your possession. Therefore we should not take (speak) any thought that we are not willing to own!

Therefore take no thought, saying, What shall we eat? or, What shall we drink? or, Wherewithal shall we be clothed? (Matthew 6:31)

In other words, what thought you speak is the thought you take!

Negative thoughts have lasting legacies...

You have to be mindful of every thought, because once you speak it, it takes on a life of its own.

Now Sarai Abram's wife bare him no children:and she had an handmaid, an Egyptian, whose name was Hagar. And Sarai said unto Abram, Behold now, the Lord hath restrained me from bearing: I pray thee, go in unto my maid; it may be that I may obtain children by her. And Abram hearkened to the voice of Sarai. And Sarai Abram's wife took Hagar her maid the Egyptian, after Abram had dwelt ten years in the land of Canaan, and gave her to her husband Abram to be his wife. And he went in unto Hagar, and she conceived: and when she saw that she had conceived, her mistress was despised in her eyes. And Sarai said unto Abram, My wrong be upon thee: I have given my maid into thy bosom; and when she saw that she had conceived, I was despised in her eyes: the Lord judge between me and thee. (Genesis 16:1-5)

169

Abraham and Sarai (Sarah) had received a promise from God but decided that He needed "help" to bring it to pass. Their plan began with a thought…, which led to a word…, which led to Ishmael…who was the father of the Arabic nation…, which was consumed by Islam…, which led to centuries of problems for Israel. Your thoughts and words can birth many lifetimes of pain!

Galatians 3:8 tells us that God preached the Gospel to Abraham before we received it. Therefore, he should have known better! When you know what God has to say about you – and because He's greater (and smarter) than you – you need to hinge everything on what He said rather than what you perceive in your circumstances!

What you say in your heart (to yourself) is important…

It's important to understand that God knows the hearts of men. He knows every thought before you think it and every word before you speak it! Now, because of Jesus, God is not judging you for your thoughts, but an un-arrested thought will lead to negative speech, which will invite the devil into your circumstances! My grandmother used to say, "…the idle mind is the devil's playground."

Anytime the devil tries to convince you God isn't real, consider the following scripture:

> *The fool hath said in his heart, There is no*
> *God. They are corrupt, they have done*

abominable works, there is none that doeth
good. (Psalms 14:1)

And when you think about who and what you are, as you contemplate your righteousness in Christ (2 Corinthians 5:21):

> *For as he thinketh in his heart, so is he: Eat*
> *and drink, saith he to thee; but his heart is*
> *not with thee. (Proverbs 23:7)*

This thought thing is so powerful – it is THE thing that cause Lucifer to rebel in pride and be condemned by God.

> *For thou hast said in thine heart, I will*
> *ascend into heaven, I will exalt my throne*
> *above the stars of God: I will sit also upon*
> *the mount of the congregation, in the sides*
> *of the north: I will ascend above the heights*
> *of the clouds; I will be like the most High.*
> *(Isaiah 14:13-14)*

Indeed, if you scratch the surface of most sin, you will find a layer of pride! If you don't deal with pride by the renewing of your mind, I can promise you, it will come back to deal with you!

It begins with the heart…

You will only manifest that which is already in you! This is why you must diligently guard your heart. You have to watch what you read. You have to screen what you watch. You have to censor what you read.

> *O generation of vipers, how can ye, being evil, speak good things? for out of the abundance of the heart the mouth speaketh. A good man out of the good treasure of the heart bringeth forth good things: and an evil man out of the evil treasure bringeth forth evil things. (Matthew 12:34-35)*

Your treasure is where your heart is, and the heart is the vessel for your treasure. If God esteems His Word above His name (Psalm 138:2), we need to be faithful to esteem that word above everything we deem to be right in our own mind!

> *Thy word have I hid in mine heart, that I might not sin against thee. (Psalms 119:11)*

Did you catch that? Meditating on God's Word will cause Jesus to be hidden (abiding) in us – and when we are hidden in Jesus and His Word is hidden in us, we become righteousness-conscious and not sin-conscious. This reduces our propensity to sin. Just like squeezing an orange will produce orange juice, we need to put God's Word in our hearts to ensure what comes out of us is good.

If you focus on foolish things, eventually you will lose your focus on righteousness. Once this happens, you will run headlong into sin.

The thought of foolishness is sin: and the scorner is an abomination to men (Proverbs 24:9)

Stand...On the promises!

When we learn to stand on what God's Word says instead of trusting on our senses – and the flawed information we get from them – we begin to see the supernatural manifest in our lives. The Bible says God will withhold no good thing from those who walk uprightly before Him (Psalm 85:11). And since you are in Christ and have his righteousness imputed to you, all the promises of God should become your expectation, not the exception.

> *For as many as are the promises of God, they all find their Yes [answer] in Him [Christ]. For this reason we also utter the Amen (so be it) to God through Him [in His Person and by His agency] to the glory of God. (2 Corinthians 1:20)*

Your confession is your profession...

In software engineering, we have a development term common to the development of user interfaces: What You See Is What You Get (WYSIWYG). But in the Kingdom, that term is What You Say Is What You Get!

> *But what saith it? The word is nigh thee, even in thy mouth, and in thy heart: that is, the word of faith, which we preach; That if*

thou shalt confess with thy mouth the Lord
Jesus, and shalt believe in thine heart that
God hath raised him from the dead, thou
shalt be saved. For with the heart man
believeth unto righteousness; and with the
mouth confession is made unto salvation.
(Romans 10:8-10)

Confessing Jesus is essential to your salvation. Indeed, the Bible also tells us we overcome not only by the Blood of Jesus, but also by the word of our testimony (Revelation 12:11). There can be no testimony without evidence or witness to an event. That said, the Word of God – when believed and trusted – produces supernatural manifestation, from which our testimony emerges.

Bottom line: Watch your thoughts, they become your words. Watch your words, they become your actions. Watch your actions, they become your habits. Watch your habits, they become your character. Watch your character; it manifests your destiny!

Therefore did my heart rejoice, and my
tongue was glad; moreover also my flesh
shall rest in hope: (Acts 2:26)

A joyous heart will produce glad speech, which will produce a sound mind, which will produce a whole body, even the Body of Christ.

SIN AND THE SAINT

On any given Sunday, you can step into many churches and hear a scathing message on sin. From these pulpits you will get a baptism of berating and get served a communion of condemnation. Sadly, millions of people consume this diet of spiritual slop every week as if it were a Biblically balanced meal.

Don't get me wrong, sin is bad and it's bad for you. But my Bible says that there is no condemnation for those who are in Christ Jesus. An improper emphasis on it is just as bad for a believer as the sin itself.

Now, as we drill into this, we need to get a working definition of sin:

No one born of God makes a practice of sinning, for God's seed abides in him, and he cannot keep on sinning because he has been born of God. By this it is evident who are the children of God, and who are the children of the devil: whoever does not practice righteousness is not of God, nor is the one who does not love his brother. (1 John 3:9-10)

I don't like to burden folks with Greek and Hebrew but it is important here in this context:

> *g0266. ἁμαρτία hamartia; from 264; a sin (properly abstract): – offence, sin (– ful).*
> *AV (174)– sin 172, sinful 1, offense 1; equivalent to 264*
> *to be without a share in*
> **to miss the mark**
> *to err, be mistaken to miss or wander from the path of uprightness and honour,*
> *to do or go wrong to wander from the law of God, violate God's law,*
> *sin that which is done wrong,*
> *sin, an offence,*
> *a violation of the divine law in thought or in act collectively,*
> *the complex or aggregate of sins committed either by a single person or by many*

The definition I want to use here is "missing the mark." Paul wrote in Philippians 3:14 that we are to press toward the mark – that is we are to keep our eyes on Jesus, focusing on Him and His righteousness. So, when you sin, your eyes are off Jesus and you run the risk of becoming sin-conscious.

(Now, I have to admit, here, that I struggled with the Scripture for this. Not because I didn't understand, but because 1 John chapter 3 is so rich with the proper teaching against sin.)

And I'm talking about SIN, not sins. Big difference – and we'll get into that in a minute.

Why, then, is preaching on sin so prevalent? Because people have been conditioned to believe feeling bad is good for you. And if you can make people feel bad enough, but convince them you have their best interest at heart, you can control them.

"But, preacher," you ask, "you gotta tell people about sin or they'll rush headlong into hell, right?"

Nope.

Here's the deal, there is only one sin that will separate anyone from God – and here it is in two passages of Scripture:

> *"For God so loved the world, that he gave his only Son, that whoever believes in him should not perish but have eternal life. For God did not send his Son into the world to condemn the world, but in order that the world might be saved through him. Whoever believes in him is not condemned, but whoever does not believe is condemned*

already, because he has not believed in the name of the only Son of God. (John 3:16-18)

However, I am telling you nothing but the truth when I say it is profitable (good, expedient, advantageous) for you that I go away. Because if I do not go away, the Comforter (Counselor, Helper, Advocate, Intercessor, Strengthener, Standby) will not come to you [into close fellowship with you]; but if I go away, I will send Him to you [to be in close fellowship with you].

And when He comes, He will convict and convince the world and bring demonstration to it about sin and about righteousness (uprightness of heart and right standing with God) and about judgment: About sin, because they do not believe in Me [trust in, rely on, and adhere to Me]; About righteousness (uprightness of heart and right standing with God), because I go to My Father, and you will see Me no longer; About judgment, because the ruler (evil genius, prince) of this world [Satan] is judged and condemned and sentence already is passed upon him. (John 16:8-11 AMP)

Denying Jesus is the only sin that will separate anyone from God. Period. This is the only sin that God will hold against anyone. This is THE sin!

Now, before anyone goes bringing up Luke 12:10 regarding blasphemy against the Holy Spirit, I humbly submit that if you deny Jesus, you have effectively blasphemed the Holy Spirit.

God's Word clearly says that He will remember our sins no more (Hebrews 8:12, 10:17), so it is clear that He will not punish you for what He has already forgotten! Those are "the sins."
Man that's good news.

The bad news is your individual sins will judge themselves.

Get caught in a lie and your integrity is tainted.

Get caught in adultery and your marriage will be damaged.

Get caught stealing and you risk criminal prosecution.

Kill someone and you have destroyed the image and likeness of God.

Suffice it to say that God isn't thrilled with any of these. And, contrary to popular belief, Grace is not a license to do any of these things. Paul wrote in 1 Corinthians 10:23 that all things are lawful (that means you CAN do them) but all things are not expedient (some things you SHOULDN'T do). But, if you're righteousness-conscious, you'll avoid more wrong by accident than you ever would on-purpose by being sin-conscious!

In other words, you'll find yourself more on target than you will missing the mark!

179

Just like there is no basketball player that makes every shot…

No baseball player who hits every ball or makes every catch…

Sometimes you miss. That's it.

The good news is that if you hit the MAJOR target – you made the team! And your coach will always be there to help you constantly improve – he will never berate you for missing the mark because He redeemed and restored you, not criticized and condemned you!

Just. That. Simple.

So, when you miss, don't get down in the doldrums about it and become sin-conscious. Repent! Turn away from what is harmful and return to your righteousness in Christ.

WORKING OUT YOUR SALVATION

The Bible is very clear on whether or not we are saved by works. Line upon line, precept upon precept tells us that it is only by Grace through Faith that we are saved.

Scripture is equally clear that salvation is the Gift of God – and that it is freely given and there is nothing any of us can do to earn or attain it. It is the Gift of God giving Himself to us (Ephesians 2:8)

This passage is one upon which many in the Body of Christ too easily choke upon:

> *Therefore, my beloved, as you have always*
> *obeyed, so now, not only as in my presence*
> *but much more in my absence, work out*

your own salvation with fear and trembling,
13) for it is God who works in you, both to
will and to work for his good pleasure.
(Philippians 2:12-13)

Work out your own salvation. Proponents of religion and adherents to the law will insist this means you have to do something to maintain your salvation, as if it were progressive instead of permanent.

James is very clear in telling us that faith without works is dead (James 2:14-17). This passage of Scripture, too, is frequently used to yoke Saints under the bondage of works. What this passage of Scripture really means that only a living tree will bear fruit. In other words, fruit is the evidence of life in the tree. So, if you have living, active faith inside you, good works will manifest from it.

Let's break "works" down into two categories: Works of the flesh and manifestation of the Spirit.

Works of the flesh are simply this: when you are operating in your own power. You and your works cannot save yourself and neither can the law. If either were the case, Jesus wouldn't be necessary. And since salvation is a free gift that you neither deserved, nor could you obtain on your own, there is no effort on your part required to maintain it.

Manifestation of the Spirit is this: When the Holy Spirit abides (dwells, is alive, and active) in you, He begins to change you from the inside out. Your attitude and behavior reflects that active change agent within you.

So, when you work out your salvation, you are demonstrating the activity of the Holy Spirit dwelling in you, which manifests in godly actions.

We have to remember that works are a fruit (expression) of salvation, not a root (prerequisite) of it!

So, let's take a look at "fear and trembling," shall we...

Here's what Paul said to Timothy concerning fear:

> *For God did not give us a spirit of timidity (of cowardice, of craven and cringing and fawning fear), but [He has given us a spirit] of power and of love and of calm and well-balanced mind and discipline and self-control. (2 Timothy 1:7, AMP)*

Clearly, God is not behind fear. Fear is the absence of Faith! Fear is an indicator of spiritual poverty.

If God is not the author of fear, what is Paul speaking of? Let me help you out: Respect or reverence.

> *The fear of the Lord is the beginning of knowledge; fools despise wisdom and instruction. (Proverbs 1:7)*

No good parent wants their children to fear them – that would be invoking a terrorist spirit. But every parent wants their children to love and to honor them. My sons know my name but they call me "Dad." That is a form of reverence and respect. However, they trust that I have their best interest at heart and know that I would never do anything to hurt them.

Jesus is the best example for understanding the heart of God. Remember, He is the express image of the Father (Hebrews 1:3) and if you've seen Him you've seen the Father (John 14:9).

Watch this: Jesus never sent anyone away. Jesus never told anyone to cower and fear. Jesus never told anyone to run and hide. If we really want to understand what "fear of the Lord" means, we should look to Jesus. He always extends the invitation:

Come. Come unto me. Follow me. Come and see.

So, here are the pieces we have so far, we are to manifest, express, or display our salvation with reverence and respect for the one who saved us. But, still, there is a missing part:

Love.

Remember, if we have no love, we are not Jesus' disciples (John 13:35). If we have no love, we are and have nothing (1 Corinthians 13:1-3).

I want to repeat verse 12 of this chapter's core text from the Amplified:

> *Therefore, my dear ones, as you have always obeyed [my suggestions], so now, not only [with the enthusiasm you would show] in my presence but much more*

because I am absent, work out (cultivate, carry out to the goal, and fully complete) your own salvation with reverence and awe and trembling (self-distrust, with serious caution, **tenderness of conscience***, watchfulness against temptation, timidly shrinking from* **whatever might offend God** *and discredit the name of Christ). (Philippians 2:12, emphasis mine)*

Now some might say, "well, preacher, that just contradicts what you just said about fear."

No, it doesn't, and here's why. We have to let scripture interpret Scripture. Scripture says we are to go boldly before the throne of Grace (Hebrews 4:16). You cannot be bold and timid at the same time. And we already established that fear is not from God.

I want to focus your attention on the two highlighted points in the text:

First, "tenderness of conscience." This comes from having the mind of Christ. And the mind of Christ is God's unconditional Love and Grace. This is righteousness-consciousness. This means manifesting your righteousness and not dragging your sins around with you.

Second, "whatever might offend God." Let me stop here and say that every offense against God was satisfied at the cross. He said He'd remember our sins no more (Hebrews 8:12, 10:17). So, how do we offend God? When we deny what Jesus did for us. For the sinner, that's to deny that Jesus died for the sins of mankind – which, by the way is

185

the only sin that sends anyone to hell. For the saint, on the other hand, we offend God when we deny the Grace of God – that is, when we return to the law.

When you love someone, you will seek to see things from their point-of-view. When you love someone, you'll go out of your way not to offend them or provoke them to anger. When you love someone, even a rebuke will be given with compassion. God's point of view is Love – and it should be ours.

So, to fully assemble this, we are to manifest, express, or display our salvation with reverence and respect for the one who saved us, demonstrating our love for the one who saved us by sharing this love with others.

I want to wrap this up with the second verse of the text:

> 13) *for it is God who works in you, both to*
> *will and to work for his good pleasure.*

If you really want to work out your own salvation, stop working and start resting! Stop trying and start trusting!

It is the Holy Spirit dwelling in you that brings about the change in your life. When you rest from your labor, you let the Holy Spirit do the work of pruning, purging, shaping, and molding. Like we said last week, present your body as a living sacrifice – turn it over to God and let him use it.

Your salvation is a done deal – there's nothing more you can do than you did when you received it! You don't have to prove anything to God; you're accepted in the beloved.

You didn't have to work to get saved and you don't have to work to stay saved! This victory is won on the battlefield of the mind.

THE BATTLE FOR THE MIND

At the end of the day, satan only has one weapon at his disposal: deception. And because your born-again spirit is just like Jesus', he can only attack you on two of the three fronts of your being – your soul and your body.

You know, like God is tripartite – Father, Son, and Holy Spirit – we have three parts as well: spirit, soul, and body. Each of these parts represents a discrete battleground and the devil is well aware that he cannot touch the born-again spirit because it is of the same substance as God.

The soul consists of four components: mind, will, intellect, and emotion. If you think of your soul as a "nation," the mind would be its "capital." In other words, the mind is the seat of the soul. If we look at this from a military perspective, the mind becomes the greatest battlefield in history.

The Bible tells us that we are not to be conformed to this world – that is, shaped by it – but to be transformed by the renewing of our minds.

> *And be not conformed to this world: but be ye transformed by the renewing of your mind, that ye may prove what is that good, and acceptable, and perfect, will of God. (Romans 12:2)*

I have to point out here, that the suffix "-ing" suggests a reiterative process. Anytime you see "-ing" in scripture, it means to do it continuously. But I digress…

One of the key (and worst) ways we become conformed to the world is by accepting things from the devil as if they are from God. Sickness, natural disasters, poverty, oppression, and bondage are not from God.

However, the devil loves to have people – especially the saints – ascribe bad things to God. Even insurance and indemnity companies refer to calamities as "acts of God." Why? Because submitting to calamity ensures you will not resist it! But you cannot resist the devil if you are not first submitted to God – and you cannot be submitted to God with an un-renewed mind!

Submit yourselves therefore to God. Resist the devil, and he will flee from you. (James 4:7)

Conformation takes place when external forces reshape us but transformation occurs when we are reshaped from within. As I mentioned earlier, the born-again spirit is re-created in the image of Christ...

> *Therefore if any man be in Christ, he is a new creature: old things are passed away; behold, all things are become new. (2 Corinthians 5:17)*

That said, our objective must be to get our soul and our flesh aligned with our spirits – or at least get them going in the same direction!

One of the "churchenese" sayings is that of "Carnal Christians." This is commonly used to describe "sinful Christians." When I say "churchenese," I'm speaking of those things that sound spiritual but have no real Biblical foundation. To that point, there is no such thing as a "sinful Christian;" you are either a sinner or saint – you can't be both! Jesus said that we are to abide in Him and His Word is to abide in us (John 15:4-7), and if we abide in Him, we are sinless!

> *5 And ye know that he was manifested to take away our sins; and in him is no sin. 6 Whosoever abideth in him sinneth not: whosoever sinneth hath not seen him, neither known him. (1 John 3:5-6)*

190

Now, don't get it twisted, I'm not saying that we cannot or do not sin – as long as we are in flesh, we are subject to worldly input. However, when our born-again spirits lead us – quickened to righteousness – we do not set out to sin!

As for what is carnal, consider the following from Strong's:

> **g4561**. σάρξ *sarx; probably from the base of 4563; flesh (as stripped of the skin), i. e. (strictly) the meat of an animal (as food), or (by extension) the body (as opposed to the soul (or spirit), or as the symbol of what is external, or as the means of kindred), or (by implication) human nature (with its frailties (physically or morally) and passions), or (specially), a human being (as such):– carnal (– ly, +– ly minded), flesh (– ly). AV (151)– flesh 147, carnal 2, carnally minded +g5427 1, fleshly 1; flesh (the soft substance of the living body, which covers the bones and is permeated with blood) of both man and beasts the body the body of a man used of natural or physical origin, generation or relationship born of natural generation the sensuous nature of man, " the animal nature" without any suggestion of depravity the animal nature with cravings which incite to sin the physical nature of man as subject to suffering a living creature (because possessed of a body of flesh) whether man or beast the flesh, denotes mere human nature, the earthly nature of*

man apart from divine influence, and therefore prone to sin and opposed to God

"Carnal" has the same root word found in "chili con carne," or "chili with meat." A carnal mind is driven by the flesh. In other words, to be carnally minded is to be a meathead! There are no meatheads who are true Kingdom citizens!

And if you continue in "meat-headedness," you will wind up being a "dead head!"

> *6 For to be carnally minded is death; but to be spiritually minded is life and peace. 7 Because the carnal mind is enmity against God: for it is not subject to the law of God, neither indeed can be. 8 So then they that are in the flesh cannot please God. (Romans 8:6-8)*

This is why renewing the mind is so important. Because you come into the world with input from your five natural senses, it is your natural inclination to trust that input. And without constant renewing (prayer, Word Study, fellowship) your mind will tend toward carnality.

Here's the good news, though! Just like darkness is not the opposite of light – it is the absence of it, the carnal mind is not the opposite of the mind of Christ – it is the absence of it. In other words, the mind of Christ will displace your meat-headedness and give life to the dead-meat of your flesh!

14 But the natural man receiveth not the things of the Spirit of God: for they are foolishness unto him: neither can he know them, because they are spiritually discerned. 15 But he that is spiritual judgeth all things, yet he himself is judged of no man. 16 For who hath known the mind of the Lord, that he may instruct him? But we have the mind of Christ. (1 Corinthians 2:14-16)

As part of the "believers' benefits package," if you will, we obtain the mind of Christ. That's some good Gospel news! But, like any other benefit – natural or spiritual, you must appropriate it! It is only valuable if you use it! And you can only use it if you choose to:

Let this mind be in you, which was also in Christ Jesus: (Philippians 2:5)

Did you catch that? Let=permit! Therefore, we must permit the mind of Christ to displace the carnal mind – it is a choice! God is not a puppeteer and He will not force anything upon us. Just like God made every material resource available in the Garden of Eden for the first Adam, He has made every spiritual gift (in addition to the material, I might add) available through the last Adam (Jesus).

Now, to dovetail all this and drive the point home, if you don't have the mind of Christ you cannot discern or access the things of God. And if you are operating as a "meat-head," well, the devil is more than happy to provide the seasoning to prepare you for his devouring! Guarding your mind is essential because it is the gateway to your heart. And unless we get our mind lined up with the spirit, the rest of the soulish part of our being will follow the flesh. In this lifetime, we may not experience perfection with the alignment of our souls and flesh with our spirits. However, if we can get our minds aligned with our spirits – and get the rest of our soulish realm to fall in line – we get a two-on-one mismatch! I like those numbers…what about you?

Once you realize you have the numbers in your favor, it's easy to face down your fears!

FACING DOWN FEAR

I saw a meme on Facebook saying that there are 365 instances of the words "Fear Not" in the Bible. The author of this meme supposes that there is one "Fear Not" for every day of the year. I had to research this for myself; I once made the mistake of actually saying this in a Sunday message before I actually researched it. Here's what I found:

"Fear Not" 63 occurrences
"No Fear" 4 occurrences
"Fear" 385 occurrences

Fear is a pervasive tool of religion. And the instruction to eliminate fear from our lives is a recurring theme in Scripture. There are a lot of places in the Bible that we could springboard from on this but I'll start here:

For God hath not given us the spirit of fear;
but of power, and of love, and of a sound
mind. (2 Timothy 1:7)

And, just for emphasis, here is the same passage of Scripture in the Amplified:

For God did not give us a spirit of timidity
(of cowardice, of craven and cringing and
fawning fear), but [He has given us a spirit]
of power and of love and of calm and well–
balanced mind and discipline and self–
control. (2 Timothy 1:7)

Franklin Delano Roosevelt, the 32nd President of the United States, famously said, "…the only thing we have to fear is fear, itself." While this is not Biblical, it is true, nonetheless. How is that?

It is true because fear is a spirit. Scientifically speaking, nature abhors a vacuum and where faith is absent, fear finds a home.

How do you deal with any spirit not of God? With the Word of God, of course!

Fear and worry are common to humanity but they are unnatural responses to life's situations. Don't believe me? Fear and worry lead to stress, which leads to a myriad of physical, emotional, and mental ailments.

We are fearful of the unknown. We are fearful of the powerful. We are fearful of the hateful. Yes, we are

196

fearful of all these things but there are two persistent things we are fearful of; one of which will surprise you:

The first is the fear of failure.

This one is easy; no one likes to fail. We miss opportunities to start businesses, to engage in relationships, to invest, because the potential of failure grips us in fear. Jesus' disciples did not speak to the storm in Mark chapter 4 because they feared the storm would persist. Jesus had already given them authority to speak to situations and had demonstrated this power on numerous occasions. The disciples could not cast the demon out of the boy in Mark chapter 9 because they feared failure.

The second is the fear of success.

Yes, we are fearful of what riches and fame success will bring us. But, in the Body of Christ, many of us are fearful that we may do something so spectacular for God that it will bring us undue attention. Peter, at the behest of Jesus, stepped out of a ship onto a raging sea to join Jesus, who was walking on the water in Matthew 14. He stepped out in faith and began to walk on the water, himself. However, he was soon overcome by the prevailing storm and began to sink. I submit to you that Peter not only feared the storm but he feared that he might actually be successful at something Jesus did.

Now, most people would think that because fear steps in where faith is absent that faith is the solution. To that, I'd say you are partially correct.

The remedy for fear is Love.

Love, love, and more love. To borrow from a Frankie Beverly song, Love is the Key! Faith is definitely important but the Bible makes it plain:

> *For [if we are] in Christ Jesus, neither circumcision nor uncircumcision counts for anything, but only faith activated and energized and expressed and working through love. (Galatians 5:5 AMP)*

Faith works by love. An engine without fuel is little more than an expensive paperweight or an overwrought boat anchor. Love is what is needed to fuel faith!

The biggest reason why folks stumble in their faith walk is because they are hobbled in love. Unforgiveness, bitterness, envy, and bigotry all are hindrances to love. And, because God is love, and faith is powered by love, and without faith, it is impossible to please God; we cannot fully appropriate God's promises because they are obtained by faith, which works by love!

Got it?

Here's what the Bible says about Love concerning fear:

> *There is no fear in love, but perfect love casts out fear. For fear has to do with punishment, and whoever fears has not been perfected in love. (1 John 4:18)*

Mature love displaces fear. The more mature your love is the more powerful your faith becomes!

But watch that second part: "For fear has to do with punishment."

When you catch that, it changes your whole paradigm for soul-winning and discipleship!

Preaching hellfire and damnation only brings about fear but only love will cast out fear!

If you find yourself in fear, find a way to express the Love of God to someone.

If it doesn't work, increase the dosage until fear is gone!

The Bible tells us that we are empowered to go boldly before the throne of Grace – if we can do that, we have absolutely nothing to fear!

We extinguish the flames of fear by turning on the fire hose of love.

When you've extinguished the flames of fear, you can walk in confidence even when it seems life, itself, is out to get you.

WHY ME

hy me?

This is one of the most profound questions ever asked by anyone living or dead.

It would be easy to draw from the Scriptures and conclude that God rains on the Just and the unjust.

> *So that you may be sons of your Father who is in heaven. For he makes his sun rise on the evil and on the good, and sends rain on the just and on the unjust. (Matthew 5:45)*

It would be equally easy to draw from the passage of Scripture that alludes to "…The Lord gives and the Lord taketh away." (Job 1:21)

The use of the former is apropos; the latter has been routinely abused.

> *I will not leave you comfortless: I will come*
> *to you. Yet a little while, and the world seeth*
> *me no more; but ye see me: because I live,*
> *ye shall live also. At that day ye shall know*
> *that I am in my Father, and ye in me, and I*
> *in you. (John 14:18-20)*

Some people like to see themselves as pawns in God's chess game with the devil. They equate suffering with piety and will frequently be the ones to ask:

Why not me?

These are the folks who count it as a badge of honor that God "chose" them to suffer for his sake. They believe that God heaped calamity on them to teach them a lesson.

They say, like Job, "…the Lord giveth and the Lord taketh away…"

Well…

That's well intended but not true. God gives. Period. The Bible tells us that every good gift comes from God:

> *Every good gift and every perfect gift is from*
> *above, and cometh down from the Father of*
> *lights, with whom is no variableness, neither*
> *shadow of turning. (James 1:17)*

and that all his gifts are without repentance

For the gifts and calling of God are without repentance. (Romans 11:29)

Life is a gift and God doesn't take it. Jesus made this abundantly clear:

The thief cometh not, but for to steal, and to kill, and to destroy: I am come that they might have life, and that they might have it more abundantly. (John 10:10)

Let's play a game of "connect-the-dots…"

Jesus said, "If you've seen me, you've seen the Father…" (John 14:9)

He said, "The Son only does what He sees the Father do…" (John 5:19)

He said, "I come do do the will of He who sent me…" (John 6:38)

He also said, "I and the Father are one…" (John 10:30)

And the Author of Hebrews said, "Jesus is the express image of the Father…" (Hebrews 1:3)

So, here are a few key questions:

During Jesus' earthly ministry (Matthew, Mark, Luke, and John)…

How many people did Jesus make sick? None!

How many did He cause to die? None!

How many people did He heap calamity upon? None!

But, watch this, He healed all who came to him…

And the only three he didn't stop death from taking?

He raised them from the dead.

The Bible says, it is not God's will that any perish but that they all come to repentance (2 Peter 3:3)…

That means He wants to see EVERYONE saved! That "saved" comes from the Greek word, "sozo," which is commonly interpreted to mean "salvation from sin."

But it is a multifaceted word that also means:

- Delivered from demonic oppression
- Bodily healing
- And material blessing (prosperity)

All of the above constitute the will of God

So why doesn't everyone get saved?

Some because they reject the Gospel…

Some because God has bad PR people…

So why doesn't everyone get healed?

I don't know…but it ain't God's fault!

We are created in the image of God to look like him and the likeness of God to act like him. We are his ambassadors – we are to reflect the will, culture, and intent of His Kingdom.

People often say, well it was just God's timing and He never makes a mistake. And that's absolutely true. But I want to make something perfectly clear, that the devil's timing is awful and he is the very absence of perfection. His aim is terrible and his motives are evil.

I've got good news for you: It is no sin to ask, "why me?" Asking that question simply reveals your humanity and your awareness that you don't have all the answers.

But it's foolish to ask, "why not me?" See, when you ask this question, you tempt God, which you should never do. It is also false humility – and when you scratch the paint of false humility, you find a veneer of pride.

We all must launch out fearlessly where God sends us. The waves will toss us and our boat will be rocked – but Jesus is with you resting in the boat! So, you can have confidence that you'll make it to the other side!

I don't know what you're going through but the Jesus who was in the boat with the disciples is in yours, too.

And He's doing the same thing He was doing in their boat…

Resting.

So, if God is resting in you, you don't need to worry. Worry doesn't increase tomorrow's peace; it robs today of its joy!

You need to know that God is the solution to your problem, not the source of your problems.

You will never be the target of His wrath, because that was laid upon Jesus. God will never woo you to turn around and wound you!

As you go through the storms of life, you need to know this:

Sometimes God calms the storm and sometimes He calms His child.

You'll fully enjoy that peace when what you say about yourself lines up with what God says about you!

WHO DO YOU SAY YOU ARE?

One of the things we, as Christians, have to come to the realization of is our identity in Christ. I have come to the conclusion that there is no more important piece of Kingdom knowledge than this.

Jesus asked His disciples two questions, who did people say He was and who did they say He was:

> *13 Now when Jesus went into the region of Caesarea Philippi, He asked His disciples, Who do people say that the Son of Man is? 14 And they answered, Some say John the Baptist; others say Elijah; and others Jeremiah or one of the prophets. 15 He said to them, But who do you [yourselves] say*

that I am? 16 Simon Peter replied, You are the Christ, the Son of the living God. 17 Then Jesus answered him, Blessed (happy, fortunate, and to be envied) are you, Simon Bar– Jonah. For flesh and blood [men] have not revealed this to you, but My Father Who is in heaven. 18 And I tell you, you are Peter [Greek, Petros –a large piece of rock], and on this rock [Greek, petra –a huge rock like Gibraltar] I will build My church, and the gates of Hades (the powers of the infernal region) shall not overpower it [or be strong to its detriment or hold out against it. (Matthew 16:13-18 AMP)

This question is important to you, too because it is key in understanding earthly identity.

I remember growing up, my Mom would always tell me, "Be Yourself." However, as unique as you may be, you are shaped by the individuals and environment surrounding you. I suffered from an identity crisis because I neither identified with the people around me nor my environment. As a result, I spent most of my youth grappling for understanding.

I was confused.

I learned a valuable lesson in my struggle, though: I could allow myself to be shaped by my circumstances (being conformed to them) or I could shape my own identity by what I've observed (being transformed). This helped me to really process Romans 12:2.

When I began to grow a relationship with my heavenly Father through Jesus, I learned something even more important.

It was what He said about me that really counted. It wasn't what teachers, relatives, military superiors, lovers, or even my parents said about me.

I am loved (John 3:16)

I am saved (Romans 10:9)

I am delivered (Luke 11:4)

I am healed (1 Peter 2:24)

I am prospered (2 Corinthians 9:8)

I am protected (John 16:33)

It was here that I learned the true meaning of humility: Agreeing with what God says about me.

What other people say about me ain't my business. What they say about you ain't your business.

If you only know that God exists and that you must worship and obey Him, all you have is religion. However, if you understand His heart and mind toward you, that is the beginning of a relationship.

And let me tell you this, you will never get what you need from religion. All religion will do is tear you down and wear you out. Relationship with the Father through Jesus will refresh, revive, restore, and even resurrect you.

Some of us had the influence of great parents growing up. Some of us had a great environment.

Some of us had neither – and, believe it or not, that's okay.

Why? Because either you *have* Jesus or you *can have* Him!

It's your NOW that will define your TOMORROW, not your YESTERDAY!

He will heal the wounds. He will fix the cracks. He will mend the breaks. He will fill the holes.

Jesus was telling His disciples that what people thought of Him wasn't important – it was what *they* thought of Him.

Likewise, it isn't what people say about you that's important, it's what God says about you. And when you absorb what God says about you, you will change what you say and think about you!

RECONSTRUCTING HEALING

Y ou cannot let just anyone lay hands on you or pray for you! If the person who wants to pray over you or a loved one during an illness is not fully persuaded of not only God's *ABILITY* to heal, but also of His *WILLINGNESS*, you may have to politely decline their request.

A walk through of Mark 5:35-42 is in order. Here we find Jairus seeking Jesus to obtain healing for his daughter...

> *35 While he yet spake, there came from the ruler of the synagogue's house certain which said, Thy daughter is dead: why troublest thou the Master any further?*

A bad diagnosis is a FACT but God's Word is TRUTH (1 Peter 2:24). A doctor may diagnose you with an illness (fact) but the Word of God says you're healed (truth)! We must learn to subordinate facts to truth!

> *36 As soon as Jesus heard the word that was spoken, he saith unto the ruler of the synagogue, Be not afraid, only believe.*

Fear is the ABSENCE of faith. We have to TRUST that God's Word is infallible and that His promises are appropriated by faith (Hebrews 11:6, 2 Peter 1:4)

> *37 And he suffered no man to follow him, save Peter, and James, and John the brother of James.*

Jesus had TWELVE disciples but He only permitted THREE to go with Him. You may be surrounded by saved folk but they may not be equipped for a faith fight. When unshakeable faith is necessary, anyone who is not in faith with you may be excess baggage.

> *38 And he cometh to the house of the ruler of the synagogue, and seeth the tumult, and them that wept and wailed greatly.*

Those around you will either agree with the circumstances or the prevailing truth. Not everyone among you is with you (Job 1:6)!

39 And when he was come in, he saith unto them, Why make ye this ado, and weep? the damsel is not dead, but sleepeth.

The Word of God (Jesus) speaks power over circumstances. You should, too!

40 And they laughed him to scorn. But when he had put them all out, he taketh the father and the mother of the damsel, and them that were with him, and entereth in where the damsel was lying.

Even some saved folks don't believe in God's willingness to heal. However, as Jesus is the express image of the Father (Hebrews 1:3) and – in examining the Gospels – Jesus was not only willing but actually healed ALL (Matthew 4:24, 8:16, 12:15, Luke 4:40, 6:17, 6:19, 8:43, 8:41), we must conclude it is ALWAYS God's will to heal. Now, before some of you say, "Preacher, why isn't everyone healed?", let me say it is God's will that everyone is saved (2 Peter 2:9) yet not everyone is.

Give that one a minute to sink in before reading further...

41 And he took the damsel by the hand, and said unto her, Talitha cumi; which is, being interpreted, Damsel, I say unto thee, arise.

One Word from God can change anything. Notice here Jesus did not go into a lengthy prayer, "binding and loosing," and so forth; rather He simply exercised His authority. He is our example and He did not beg, plead, or tarry, saying, "...if it be your will," and neither should we. Jesus has given us AUTHORITY over the ABILITY of the enemy (Luke 10:19). We are COMMANDED to heal the sick (Luke 10:9).

> *42 And straightway the damsel arose, and walked; for she was of the age of twelve years. And they were astonished with a great astonishment.*

When The Kingdom of God shows up, the miraculous happens. This must be our EXPECTATION, not the EXCEPTION! Jesus told us that we'd do Greater Works (in number, not magnitude – don't get it twisted) but we cannot if we are unwilling to stand on the Word and exercise the dominion authority Jesus restored to us.

We need to stand on and exercise this authority because religion has persuaded the world that sickness, pain, and poverty are part of the chastisement of God. Nothing could be further from the truth!

PAUL'S THORN AND THE CHASTENING OF GOD

I stand on the premise that God WILL NOT make you sick to chasten you and that anyone who teaches that is repeating a lie straight from the pit of hell.

Yep, I said it!

I believe this is a revelation that will cause religious shackles to fall off the hearts and minds of all who receive it!

214

Strong words, for sure, but words of necessity. You see the church has been bound by a doctrine that suggests that God is the architect of illness and that He afflicts His children to chasten them. Many teachers have used Paul's thorn as a means of demystifying why bad things happen to good people. There are many scriptures proffered in support of that theory, chief of which is the following:

> *And lest I should be exalted above measure*
> *through the abundance of the revelations,*
> *there was given to me a thorn in the flesh,*
> *the messenger of Satan to buffet me, lest I*
> *should be exalted above measure. For this*
> *thing I besought the Lord thrice, that it*
> *might depart from me. And he said unto me,*
> *My grace is sufficient for thee: for my*
> *strength is made perfect in weakness. Most*
> *gladly therefore will I rather glory in my*
> *infirmities, that the power of Christ may rest*
> *upon me. Therefore I take pleasure in*
> *infirmities, in reproaches, in necessities, in*
> *persecutions, in distresses for Christ's sake:*
> *for when I am weak, then am I strong. (2*
> *Corinthians 12:7-10)*

Now, we must first understand that Paul referred to himself as a Pharisee (Acts 26:5, Philippians 3:5). He was well schooled in the law, having studied at the feet of Gamaliel. Before his encounter with the risen Jesus, I posit that the former Saul of Tarsus was quite proud of his educational accomplishments. Perhaps God dealt with Paul to keep him from being puffed-up in the knowledge

215

of the Kingdom of God as He was in his knowledge of the law.

Now, I'll admit, that's speculation and can be considered Eisegesis. However, we can glean something concrete from the text that Paul's thorn in the flesh was a messenger of satan sent to buffet him. A disease or an infirmity is not a messenger. This passage is referring to a sprit being – or a natural being under the influence of a spirit being – that satan unleashed to impede Paul's progress in spreading the Gospel. Furthermore, when Paul spoke of infirmities in verse 10, he was simply saying that whatever he had to endure for the Gospel's sake, he was willing to take.

This is Paul's testimony, saint, not yours! But I digress.

Nearly everywhere you look in Scripture, thorns refer to people:

Thorns are meant to bring pain (Genesis 3:17-19 ESV).

Thorns will invade your world (Numbers 33:55).

Thorns will trap and enslave you (Joshua 23:13).

Thorns will waste your time (2 Samuel 23:6-7).

Thorns will bring about the spirit of fear (Ezekiel 2:6).

Thorns threaten your harvest (Hebrews 6:4-8).

216

John 10:10 states that, "the thief comes to steal, kill, and destroy." Who is the thief? Why, the devil, of course; that is his mission. When something comes about that steals from you or tries to kill you or tries to destroy your life, you can be sure that this is the devil and that God is far from it. Indeed, Jesus identifies his role in the life of the believer in the same passage of scripture, stating that, "I am come that they may have life more abundantly."

Now, my first question to the reader is, "Is there anything abundant about sickness or bodily affliction?"

I'll help you out: NO!

If you are a Christ-conscious believer, you are an heir to the promises of Abraham and have an earnest expectation of long, healthy life.

> *And these are the days of the years of Abraham's life which he lived, an hundred threescore and fifteen years. Then Abraham gave up the ghost, and died in a good old age, an old man, and full of years; and was gathered to his people. (Genesis 25:7-8)*

Let's face it, pain and suffering is stressful and certainly not conducive to long life. Further, it is not the will of God that His children, the saints, go through life this way. I've posed this question many times but it begs to be asked again in this context, would you, a parent, afflict your child with so much as a tummy-ache to get them to behave properly? I believe the answer to that is, "NO!"

And if God is a better parent than any of us could aspire to be, why would He do such a thing? The answer is, He will not!

Psalm 103:3 Puts it thusly:

> *Who forgiveth all thine iniquities; who healeth all thy diseases.*

What part of ALL is unclear, here? God heals – period!

For the icing on the cake, let's take a look at Jesus. Matthew 4:24 and 8:15, and Luke 6:19, all clearly state that Jesus healed all who come to them. It is interesting to note that these people whom He healed were Old Covenant saints – they had neither the risen Christ nor the Holy Spirit! BUT YOU DO!

Another good question is, how many people did Jesus make sick during His earthly ministry? Again, the answer is clearly NONE!

> *Then answered Jesus and said unto them, Verily, verily, I say unto you, The Son can do nothing of himself, but what he seeth the Father do: for what things soever he doeth, these also doeth the Son likewise. (John 5:19)*

Then, If Jesus only healed folks and made none sick (and certainly didn't kill anyone), and He only did what He saw the Father do, this means God makes no one sick! But let's

218

take it a step further, If God did, indeed, make some sick and Jesus healed them that would make Jesus' actions contrary to the will of God, right?

When will the Body of Christ acknowledge that bodily healing is available for all believers? I'm tired of this weak-kneed, so-called "Christianity" that teaches that sickness somehow emanates from God. What part of "Jesus healed them all" (Matthew 12:15) are we missing?

I've said this before and I'll say it again, ALL means ALL, y'all!

I love how God revealed this to Isaiah:

> *But he was wounded for our transgressions, he was bruised for our iniquities: the chastisement of our peace was upon him; and with his stripes we are healed. (Isaiah 53:5)*

Note two things:

First, God said the chastisement of our peace was upon Him, that is, Jesus. This means the punishment we deserved was laid squarely on Jesus. Once we are saved and in Christ, the affliction we deserved is no longer reserved for us. Glory to God! Now this chastisement actually extends beyond the believer in that God is no longer making corporate judgments as He did with Sodom and Gomorrah. The plagues, weather phenomena, and acts of terrorism emanate from satan, not God! Yes, God did these sorts of things in the Old Testament, but they are conspicuously absent from the New Testament!

Second, the stripes (the beating, scourging, and scorning) laid upon Jesus were the payment for the health and healing of the believer! Again, those who are in Christ have the earnest expectation that the God who saved them from eternal death can save them from earthy disease, plague, and disability!

God chastens His children with His Word. This is explained in 2 Timothy 3:16:

> *All scripture is given by inspiration of God, and is profitable for doctrine, for reproof, for correction, for instruction in righteousness:*

And again, in 2 Timothy 4:2:

> *Preach the word; be instant in season, out of season; reprove, rebuke, exhort with all long suffering and doctrine.*

Correction for the believer is from the Word of God, not sickness! Man, this is a revelation!

The difference between capability and manifestation is potential. God has given us awesome capability but we have to get a revelation from Him for our potential to be revealed. The Body of Christ frequently operates beneath privilege because purpose is unknown to most of us.

220

God did not permit anything. Just like in the case of Job, there is no permissive clause where God grants permission! Because of Paul's revelation, the devil was coming after him just like he came after Job. But Paul had the Holy Spirit and the blood of Jesus, so God was able to tell him that Grace was more than enough to overcome his trouble! I believe Grace gave Paul the ability to speak against his tormentor because, through his words, he showed us how to overcome ours.

I stand firmly behind my original premise. Any teaching that discounts healing or, worse, supposes that God is the architect of sickness is a perverted Gospel. I will teach this faithfully until the Holy Spirit releases me from it. Be healed. Be set free. In Jesus' name!

I have a term for the folks who insist upon teaching that God is the source of our afflictions: "Jobians…"

JOBIAN THEOLOGY

Ⅰn this chapter, I want to take on a subject that has silently taken over a large portion of mainstream Christianity.

Jobian Theology.

Jobian theology comes from the premise that what happened to Job is greater than the finished work of Christ. Now, no Christian would ever admit to subscribing to such foolishness, but their words and deeds contradict this. By definition, a "Christian" is someone who aspires to be "like Christ." However, many "Christians" when evaluating their own lives and circumstances, see themselves more "like Job" than "like Christ," hence, "Jobians."

Job is the "poster boy" for religion. Whenever someone has to explain why bad things happen to good people, religious apologists run to Job.

First to level-set, the common assumption is that God granted permission to satan to afflict Job. Nothing could be further from the truth. First of all, God was not setting Job up to be knocked out-of-the-park by satan. The question in Job 1:8 "Have you considered my servant, Job," could be better translated "Hast thou set thine heart on," or "Hast thou given thine attention to." In other words, God was asking the devil why did he have his heart set on Job.

satan saw the blessing on Job's life and thought Job served God only because he was blessed. In fact, satan's strategy was to get God to afflict Job. It is important to note here that when Job was afflicted, it was satan, and not God, who afflicted him.

Another thing to note is how satan approached God about this. He showed up at a time when the sons of God (angels) were gathering at the throne.

> *Now there was a day when the sons of God came to present themselves before the Lord, and Satan came also among them (Job 1:6).*

He tried to conceal himself among the heavenly host. There's a lesson to be learned from this: that everyone among you isn't with you!

But back to the main point…

The next point of consideration is that Job was operating in fear. Job continually offered sacrifices for his children, whom he suspected weren't living right:

> And his sons went and feasted in their houses, every one his day; and sent and called for their three sisters to eat and to drink with them. And it was so, when the days of their feasting were gone about, that Job sent and sanctified them, and rose up early in the morning, and offered burnt offerings according to the number of them all: for Job said, It may be that my sons have sinned, and cursed God in their hearts. Thus did Job continually. (Job 1:4-5)

The proof that Job was operating in fear was revealed later:

> For the thing which I greatly feared is come upon me, and that which I was afraid of is come unto me (Job 3:25)

Nothing invites the devil into your situation more than fear. Paul said it best in his second letter to Timothy:

For God hath not given us the spirit of fear;
but of power, and of love, and of a sound
mind (2 Timothy 1:17)

I've said before that faith is the currency of the Kingdom of God. Conversely, fear is the currency of the principality of darkness. Job, like many Christians, today, failed to properly exchange his currency. As a result, he brought the will, culture, and intent of the principality of darkness into his world.

More to the point, Job was a man without a covenant. Job is the oldest book in the Bible, chronologically speaking and Job had neither the covenant of law nor the covenant of Grace. Job did not have either Jesus or the indwelling of the Holy Spirit. This made Job vulnerable, and it is proven when God makes a profound statement that has been terribly misinterpreted by theologians:

And the Lord said unto Satan, Behold, all
that he hath is in thy power; only upon
himself put not forth thine hand. (Job 1:12)

The challenge I pose here is, where is the "permissive clause?" Where does God grant satan permission to afflict Job? Let me help you, it ain't there. I've done a lot of searching and study on this, and – as near as I can figure – whenever God says "behold," it is usually followed by a truth. It is never used to grant permission to do anything. Here are some examples:

Behold, the Lord thy God hath set the land
before thee: go up and possess it, as the

225

Lord God of thy fathers hath said unto thee; fear not, neither be discouraged. (Deuteronomy 1:21)

Therefore thus saith the Lord God, Behold, I lay in Zion for a foundation a stone, a tried stone, a precious corner stone, a sure foundation: he that believeth shall not make haste. (Isaiah 28:16)

In both cases, a truth is stated but no permission is granted. In other words, what is stated in Job 1:12 ("Behold, all that he hath...") and in Job 2:6 ("Behold, he is in thine hand...") was not granting permission, it was stating a truth! It is critically important that this is seen because sin gives satan access to everyone outside covenant with God.

One thing that must be made abundantly clear, here, is that God did not grant satan access to Job – satan already had it! Job did not have a "hedge about him," that was satan's misunderstanding. However, God did raise a hedge around Job twice (Job 1:12 and 2:6) limiting what satan could do.

So, here's the million-dollar question, "Why didn't God stop all this?" Glad you asked. God can do anything but lie, fail, or violate His Word. The Psalmist tells us that God esteems His Word above His name (Psalm 138:2). Once God establish a thing by His Word, He will not do anything contrary to it. A great example of this is the concept of seedtime and harvest; God will not do anything contrary to this principle.

226

Another thing that must be clarified is that God is a good parent. Indeed, He is the most extraordinary of parents. As such, He will always do what is best for His children. That, said, would any good parent turn their child over to a known pervert to discipline them when they are out of order? Well, since God is the greatest parent and satan is the greatest pervert – in fact, he's the original pervert – God would not do that. It just doesn't add up. But God gave man dominion in the earth (Genesis 1:26-28) – dominion by which God expects us to influence our environment with His Word. Therefore, God didn't do anything about Job's situation because Job, himself, didn't do anything about his situation.

Whew. That was long winded – but I hope you caught it. If you didn't read it again (and again, if necessary) until you do!

One more thing: do you realize that God didn't actually chasten Job until near the end of the book? That's right, God didn't deal with Job until chapters 38-41 – and when He did, did He heap more afflictions upon Job? No, He chastened Job with His Word! This is consistent with 2 Timothy 3:16. In other words, the chastening for the child of God is the Word of God, not sickness, plague, oppression, pain, or poverty! And, at the end of God's chastening – and after Job repented (changed his mind) and prayed for his friends, God blessed Job with far more substance than what he had before! Man, that is Good News!

If God afflicted Job then delivered Him, God acted against Himself – and since a kingdom divided cannot stand, God cannot be divided or double-minded! Jesus came to destroy the works of the devil and empower us to do likewise (1 John 3:8). God will not use the works of the devil to chasten and afflict His children when He already sent His Son to destroy those works!

Let me say this, God doesn't miss – He does what He says and says what He does. He is perfect in every way. However, He expects us to emulate Him. Also, the Body of Christ is an interdependent vessel – every part is dependent upon other parts. In other words, the timely blessing of others may be contingent upon us being in the right place at the right time. So, when bad things happen to good people, it ain't God! Sometimes we miss it in what we pray for and decree. Other times we miss it when we miss an assignment. And, we must remember we live in a fallen world – and sometimes the devil uses the implements of this fallen world to thwart the prayers and actions of the Saints.

Bottom line, whose report will you believe? Will you trust in the finished work of Jesus, which gives us everything we need to experience abundant life (John 10:10) or will you place your trust in a statement that a mere man who suffered great loss without revelation of who stole from him (Job 1:21). Will you believe that God gives satan permission to afflict you, or will you trust that God will protect you (2 Thessalonians 3:3, 1 John 5:18)? Will you trust law, or place your trust in Grace?

In what and whom you believe determines whose you are – are you of Job or are you of Christ?

Job's situation changed when he changed his mind about God's plan. A changed mind is the source of true repentance!

REMORSE AND REPENTANCE

One of the great misunderstandings in the Christian walk is that you must confess each and every sin in order to be forgiven by God. Nothing could be further from the truth, as God knows everything in your heart and in your mind and, frankly, most of us do not have enough time to enumerate all our individual and collective sins.

> *For godly sorrow worketh repentance to salvation not to be repented of: but the sorrow of the world worketh death. (2 Corinthians 7:10)*

According to Strong's, repentance from the Greek actually means:

g3341. metanoia; from 3340; (subjectively) compunction (for guilt, including reformation); by implication, reversal (of (another's) decision): – repentance. AV (24)– repentance 24; a change of mind, as it appears to one who repents, of a purpose he has formed or of something he has done

Did you catch that? Repentance actually means a change of mind! It is not confessing sins. And, if you're conscious of your righteousness, you come to the realization that you don't have to be conscious of sin.

True repentance is a Kingdom principle and is only possible through the revelation of relationship with the Father through the person of Jesus Christ.

Or despisest thou the riches of his goodness and forbearance and longsuffering; not knowing that the goodness of God leadeth thee to repentance? (Romans 2:4)

In other words, it is God's unconditional Love and Grace that brings us to the point of repentance – not the law or any threat of punishment!

People often confuse remorse with repentance but they are mutually exclusive activities. For example, a man who physically abuses his wife may be remorseful for his actions, but without a change of mind, he's likely to do it again! A woman can change her mind about being unfaithful to her husband but without remorse, her mind is unlikely to remain changed.

It is reported the financial manipulator, Bernard Madoff, expressed remorse for his actions. However, he has expressed no sympathy for his victims and has offered no restitutions. Therefore, we must conclude that his remorse gives no indication of repentance.

In a similar circumstance, Michael Milken (also known as the "junk-bond king") was tried and convicted for misleading investors. However, Milken not only paid back many investors, but has dedicated his post-prison life and his wealth to finding a cure for cancer and helping at-risk youth.

In other words, true repentance is accompanied by remorse – but either, alone, without the other does not lead to a godly result. True repentance is born of true love, which will change your desires in such a way that you will want to go out of your way to not hurt the object of your affection. This requires a changed mind!

There are many examples of remorse in scripture that did not lead to repentance.

Judas Iscariot, the betrayer of Jesus, repented that he delivered an innocent man into the hands of evil, religious men but had no remorse.

Then Judas, which had betrayed him, when he saw that he was condemned, repented

232

himself, and brought again the thirty pieces
of silver to the chief priests and elders,
Saying, I have sinned in that I have betrayed
the innocent blood. And they said, What is
that to us? see thou to that. And he cast
down the pieces of silver in the temple, and
departed, and went and hanged himself.
(Matthew 27:3-5)

Indeed, there are examples of Scripture where it is said God, Himself, repented. Now it has to be clearly understood that God has no sin to confess!

And the Lord said, I will destroy man whom
I have created from the face of the earth;
both man, and beast, and the creeping thing,
and the fowls of the air; for it repenteth me
that I have made them. (Genesis 6:6)

The Lord repented for this: This also shall
not be, saith the Lord God. (Amos 7:6)

Since Jesus is the express image of the Father (Hebrews 1:3) and it is incumbent upon us to be more like Him, and He does not (or cannot) confess sin, we don't have to!

This is a liberating moment if you've been caught up in the notion you must confess every sin in order to maintain your salvation! The notion that you must confess every sin reeks of religion and is tainted with tradition.

233

There are some that teach that if you were to die instantly in a car crash in which you were going one MPH over the speed limit that you're doomed to hell. Where is the grace in that? Besides, Jesus paid the sin-debt once and for all for us and, as long as we have accepted him as Lord and Savior and abide in Him, our salvation is secure!

Paul wrote, thusly, in his epistle to the Romans,

> *There is therefore now no condemnation to them which are in Christ Jesus, who walk not after the flesh, but after the Spirit. (Romans 8:1)*

Indeed, Jeremiah tells us that God, Himself, will not remember our sins:

> *And no longer shall each one teach his neighbor and each his brother, saying, Know the Lord, for they shall all know me, from the least of them to the greatest, declares the Lord. For I will forgive their iniquity, and I will remember their sin no more. (Jeremiah 31:34)*

So, if God – who knows all – chooses to remember your sins no more, why would you remind him by confession?

The ability to repent is a reminder of God's perfect love for and grace toward us. Led by the Holy Spirit, repentance is the means by which we rest in righteousness – that when sin raises its head, we are able to turn from it

234

by the renewing of our mind. We do not have to confess anything to an omniscient God who has given us Jesus, who provided the remedy for sin.

There is precious little in the earth more powerful than a made-up mind. Even God said that when the people are of one mind, they can do anything (Genesis 11:6). Indeed, when folks come together with a made-up mind, the truly extraordinary can happen (Acts 2:1-2). True repentance keeps our mind stayed on Jesus, focused on righteousness and not sin. True repentance allows you to make up your mind to turn from sin and be awakened to righteousness.

It is the changed mind that leads to a changed heart that leads to a change in appearance and behavior.

APPEARANCES

As a pastor and governing body leader, I have an acute understanding of the importance some people place on appearance. Folks will judge a leader based on his or her clothes, hair, and jewelry.

As a man, people frequently misjudged me because of my hair – long and worn in dreadlocks – or the earring I frequently wear. And, I've met some Christian Brothers who, at first blush, look really radical.

What I've learned is you cannot judge anyone's holiness or righteousness by their appearance.

I've been guilty of the selfsame offense. I have looked aghast at young men with piercings, tattoos, and pants hanging down past their waistline. And, sadly, I made some terrible judgments.

Truth is, holiness is not based on appearance. Contrary to the dogma espoused by many denominations, a woman is not unholy if she wears makeup, a man is not unholy if he has long hair, and neither man not woman is unholy if they have tattoos or piercings.

Here's what the Lord, Jesus, had to say about appearances:

> *And he said unto them, Ye are they which justify yourselves before men; but God knoweth your hearts: for that which is highly esteemed among men is abomination in the sight of God. (Luke 16:15)*

Even the Old Testament warns us to avoid judging based on appearance:

> *But the Lord said unto Samuel, Look not on his countenance, or on the height of his stature; because I have refused him: for the Lord seeth not as man seeth; for man looketh on the outward appearance, but the Lord looketh on the heart. (1 Samuel 16:7)*

In other words, God is far more concerned with what's on the inside of you than what's on the outside.

Moreover, when we make judgments about people based on their outward appearance, we're not operating in love. Think about it: if you look at someone and think they're disgusting or dangerous, you will likely avoid them. That person may be someone who desperately needs to hear the good news of the Kingdom of God. Or, to make it personal, that person may be the carrier of a blessing you desperately need.

But there are those who make a big deal of outward appearances and, I humbly submit to you, that many of those are the same people that project holiness but are messed-up, inside.

The Bible warns us about people who have a form of godliness but deny God's power (2 Timothy 3:5). And, since God's power comes wrapped in love, to fail to love is to deny His power.

Furthermore, the Bible also challenges us to beware those who come in sheep's clothing:

> Beware of false prophets, which come to you
> in sheep's clothing, but inwardly they are
> ravening wolves. (Matthew 7:15)

While I'm here, it bears mentioning that you shouldn't just beware those in sheep's clothing but – and more importantly – those in shepherd's clothing!

Jesus said something about those who looked holy on the outside but were spiritually dead on the inside:

Woe unto you, scribes and Pharisees, hypocrites! for ye are like unto whited sepulchres, which indeed appear beautiful outward, but are within full of dead men's bones, and of all uncleanness. Even so ye also outwardly appear righteous unto men, but within ye are full of hypocrisy and iniquity. (Matthew 23:27-28)

Now, I'm not saying that everyone who appears holy is really jacked-up on the inside, what I'm saying is appearances can be deceiving.

The cure for judgment based on appearance is love. To fully grasp this, we go to the thirteenth chapter of 1 Corinthians.

Charity suffereth long, and is kind; charity envieth not; charity vaunteth not itself, is not puffed up, Doth not behave itself unseemly, seeketh not her own, is not easily provoked, thinketh no evil; Rejoiceth not in iniquity, but rejoiceth in the truth; Beareth all things, believeth all things, hopeth all things, endureth all things. (1 Corinthians 13:4-7)

The word "charity" actually means, "love." So, to understand this contextually and in a contemporary sense, we need to substitute the former for the latter.

Let's break this down by section.

Charity suffereth long... means love is tolerant. Contrary to popular belief, it does not mean to "endure suffering," as if love is tortuous. One of the problems with appearance-based judgment is that it lacks patience.

...and is kind... is self-explanatory. Love is kind. True love is never cruel or oppressive.

charity envieth not... Love is neither envious nor covetous.

charity vaunteth not itself, is not puffed up... True love does not call attention to itself.

Doth not behave itself unseemly... True love is never the cause of bad behavior.

seeketh not her own... True love is unselfish.

is not easily provoked... True love is neither easily offended nor quick to offend others.

thinketh no evil... True love can never be the source of evil because there is no malicious thought in true love.

Rejoiceth not in iniquity...True love neither encourages nor engages in sin

but rejoiceth in the truth;...True love is truthful

Beareth all things...True love bears the burdens of others

believeth all things...True love has no reason to doubt

hopeth all things...True love gives purpose and direction to faith

endureth all things...True love has staying power

Love is the evidence of the righteousness of God at work in the life of a believer.

RIGHTEOUSNESS REVEALED

Righteousness has so many connotations. It is a term that is often misunderstood because many – including faith-filled – folks believe it is something earned by works. But it is a gift, given to us by God, and nothing we can earn on our own.

According to 2 Corinthians 5:21, we have been made the Righteousness of God through the finished work of Jesus. In the verse immediately preceding this (5:20), it says we are ambassadors for Christ. In order to be an ambassador of any nation or kingdom, it is important that we are in right standing with the government we're representing. No nation sends out emissaries who are convicted criminals or otherwise representative of the worst elements of its citizenry!

That said, righteousness is simply right standing with God. Think of it this way, you must be in the right position to be blessed! For example, a wide receiver in football runs a specific route and positions his body to catch a pass thrown by his quarterback. Another example, when you pay your credit card bill on time each month, you position yourself to receive the bank's favor when you go to charge a purchase. The more precisely the receiver runs his route, he is in right standing with the quarterback and the more likely he is to make the catch. Likewise, paying your credit card bill on time puts you in right standing with the issuing bank.

But God is so much more! He isn't merely throwing passes, He is not just giving you money, He gave you the abundant life of Jesus (John 10:10). Because of Jesus' finished work on the cross, you have not just received a gift from God, you have received The Gift of God. (Romans 6:23).

And no man's righteousness is greater than any other man's! Isaiah wrote, our righteousness is as filthy rags (Isaiah 64:6)! It is not of our works that we are righteous lest any man should boast□ (Ephesians 2:9). It is only through the shed blood of The Lamb, slain before the foundation of time, we are made righteous! Glory to God!

We are now clothed in a robe of Righteousness. We are washed clean of our sins! When we stand before the Father, He does not see sin in us, he only sees the blood of

242

his only begotten Son! Satan may accuse us but God sees us cleansed through the blood of Jesus and simply says, "Case Dismissed!"

Because we have been made righteous, we can now – by faith – appropriate all of God's promises! We no longer have to be defeated, depressed, and dejected! We walk in victory! Thanks be to the God of Glory!!!

Now that we understand righteousness, we need to get at one of the nagging issues of religion: holiness…

HOLINESS ILLUSTRATED

If we call ourselves CHRISTIANS then we should be concerned primarily with the words and teachings of CHRIST, right? Here's what Jesus has to say about "holiness:"

NOTHING!

I have this – dare I say – revelation on teaching the Word of God: the Gospels are the foundation for ALL teaching, followed by the remainder of the New Testament (which only illuminates the person and Word of Jesus, followed by Genesis (which is God's Mission Statement), followed by the books of poetry (which are types and shadows of the Love and Wisdom of God), then the Prophets (who point to Jesus and His Kingdom)' followed by the law (what we've been delivered from because Jesus fulfilled it).

That said, the Bible says "be ye holy for I (God) am holy. Here's the bad news: YOU CAN'T BE HOLY AS GOD, NOT EVEN CLOSE. At best, your efforts will frustrate you; At worst, your works will brand you as a hypocrite!

To get to the crux of this, we need to have a knowledge of what makes God, "GOD;" at least one we can wrap our peanut brains around. Here's one thing that we can wrap our finite minds around: one of the key attributes of God is that He and his Word are one, inseparable! Because the Entire universe is suspended by the Word of His Power, the moment He violates His Word, He ceases to be "GOD" and He ceases to be Holy! So, the ONLY way we can even emulate His Holiness is to emulate how He keeps His Word. We can NEVER be as good, pure, or clean as God, but we CAN be men and women of INTEGRITY; that is, we do what we say and say what we'll do IN ALIGNMENT WITH GOD'S WORD!

Holiness does not equal righteousness. Righteousness is right standing with God made possible ONLY by the Blood of Jesus. Holiness is our conversation or LIFESTYLE – which is to be set apart and consecrated before God – but to that end, we will never be as good as God and attempts to do so start us on a slippery slope to works, effectively nullifying grace.

We cannot "do" holy without "being" holy – but holiness cannot be earned or accomplished on our own, the Blood of Jesus imparts it to us. However, to simplify: we must

245

be people of our word emulating how God and His Word are one. Because He esteems His Word above His name, He won't violate His Word. Therefore, if we are truly in Him, we'll keep our word as He keeps His Word. Holiness IS NOT what you wear, how you talk, how you wear your hair...

This vain attempt to accomplish holiness through works has resulted in the kind of religious schizophrenia that makes people run from "Christians" instead of running to Christ.

This is how we BE holy. Trying to DO holy apart from this is doomed to fail.

This is why religion leads to powerlessness. In order to fully appropriate holiness and righteousness, we need to understand the distinction between servants and sons.

SERVANTS OR SONS

One of the great debates in Christendom is the nature of our inheritance in Christ – did Jesus die to make us servants or did we become sons through Him? Someone asked me, "Does it even make a difference?" The answer is, emphatically, yes!

We were slaves under the law – before Jesus, we were slaves to sin and, by proxy, slaves to the law because the law served to reveal sin.

For we know that the law is spiritual, but I am of the flesh, sold under sin. (Romans 7:14)

Wherefore thou art no more a servant, but a son; and if a son, then an heir of God through Christ. (Galatians 4:7)

We must learn from the law, be liberated from it (not live by the law), be founded in friendship, realize we're made free by Jesus, graduate to Grace, and operate from a posture of confidence in that we're made sons of God!

Lessons of the Law

The law came about because the people did not want to hear from God directly (Exodus 19 & 20). It was not God's intent to have Moses be a mediator; it was His will to speak with the people directly. The law was never intended to make anyone holy or righteous, God gave the law to expose sin.

Wherefore then serveth the law? It was added because of transgressions, till the seed should come to whom the promise was made; and it was ordained by angels in the hand of a mediator. (Galatians 3:19)

Liberated From the Law

The only person to fully uphold the Law was Jesus and, in doing so, fulfilled it. This means He satisfied the requirements of the Law. Because the law was a curse upon mankind, Christ's fulfillment of the law set us free from the curse of the Law

> *Even as Abraham believed God, and it was accounted to him for righteousness. Know ye therefore that they which are of faith, the same are the children of Abraham. And the scripture, foreseeing that God would justify the heathen through faith, preached before the gospel unto Abraham, saying, In thee shall all nations be blessed. So then they which be of faith are blessed with faithful Abraham. For as many as are of the works of the law are under the curse: for it is written, Cursed is every one that continueth not in all things which are written in the book of the law to do them. But that no man is justified by the law in the sight of God, it is evident: for, The just shall live by faith. And the law is not of faith: but, The man that doeth them shall live in them. Christ hath redeemed us from the curse of the law, being made a curse for us: for it is written, Cursed is every one that hangeth on a tree: That the blessing of Abraham might come on the Gentiles through Jesus Christ; that we might receive the promise of the Spirit through faith. (Galatians 3:6-14)*

Found to be Friends

Friendship is a form of intimacy. True friends share their thoughts, feelings, and – often – secrets. Jesus revealed the secrets of the Kingdom of God to his disciples and, by

His written Word, to us. Some friends share a bond that is even greater than family, such as David and Jonathan.

> *Henceforth I call you not servants; for the servant knoweth not what his lord doeth: but I have called you friends; for all things that I have heard of my Father I have made known unto you. (John 15:15)*

Made Free by the Son

Some slaves have limited authority (for example, Joseph); However, Sons have the authority of the Father. Jesus said He only did what He sees the Father do (John 5:19-20). He gave his mission statement in Luke 4:18-19, to set captives free.

Unfortunately, liberty only has power when it is exercised.

It is also important to understand the revelation of liberty as it pertains to sonship because, without it, we are reduced to powerless religion instead of the empowered sainthood Jesus came to restore us to. Freedom is power – power to do the greater works Jesus commanded us to do!

> *And the servant abideth not in the house for ever: but the Son abideth ever. If the Son therefore shall make you free, ye shall be free indeed. (John 8:35-36)*

Graduating to Grace

The law was a tutor – grace is our inheritance. One of the great problems among people, in general, and in the Body of Christ is that many of us want to cling to "glory days." You know, like the high school quarterback who lives in his glory of his past and refuses to embrace the future. Likewise, there are many who find security in the Law and its ordinances. I'll never forget receiving Jesus as Lord and Savior as a teenager then being told to memorize the "Ten Commandments" in order to secure my salvation and ensure holy living.

The truth is, God wants us to grow in grace. This is why He set the "five-fold" or "five-faceted" ministry gifts in place (Ephesians 4:10-16) – to equip the saints and bring them into maturity. We mature when we understand and manifest the fullness of God's love and grace.

Because of the advent and revelation of Jesus, we are partakers of His grace and, through Him, graduates of the school of the Law.

> *Now what I mean is that as long as the inheritor (heir) is a child and under age, he does not differ from a slave, although he is the master of all the estate; But he is under guardians and administrators or trustees until the date fixed by his father. So we [Jewish Christians] also, when we were minors, were kept like slaves under [the rules of the Hebrew ritual and subject to] the elementary teachings of a system of external observations and regulations. But when the proper time had fully come, God*

251

sent His Son, born of a woman, born subject to [the regulations of] the Law, To purchase the freedom of (to ransom, to redeem, to atone for) those who were subject to the Law, that we might be adopted and have sonship conferred upon us [and be recognized as God's sons]. And because you [really] are [His] sons, God has sent the [Holy] Spirit of His Son into our hearts, crying, Abba (Father)! Father! Therefore, you are no longer a slave (bond servant) but a son; and if a son, then [it follows that you are] an heir by the aid of God, through Christ. (Galatians 4:1-7 AMP)

Secure as Sons

One of the most wonderful products of God's grace is security in our sonship. Now, I believe "once-saved-always-saved" is flawed doctrine because someone can receive Christ and later reject Him (Hebrews 6:4). In other words, you cannot lose your salvation but you can, indeed, give it away. Short of rejecting Jesus, you can always return to right relationship with the father through repentance – that is, changing your mind!

> *I will arise and go to my father, and will say unto him, Father, I have sinned against heaven, and before thee, And am no more worthy to be called thy son: make me as one of thy hired servants.*

(NOTE: This is what religion wants you to believe)

252

And he arose, and came to his father. But when he was yet a great way off, his father saw him, and had compassion, and ran, and fell on his neck, and kissed him. And the son said unto him, Father, I have sinned against heaven, and in thy sight, and am no more worthy to be called thy son. But the father said to his servants, Bring forth the best robe (symbol of relationship), and put it on him; and put a ring on his hand (symbol of authority), and shoes on his feet (symbol of inheritance): And bring hither the fatted calf, and kill it; and let us eat, and be merry: For this my son was dead, and is alive again; he was lost, and is found. And they began to be merry. (Luke 15:18-24)

The father of the prodigal son neither decried his departure nor resisted his return; rather he anticipated his arrival. This is how our Heavenly Father looks at every lost soul. God stands at His gate daily awaiting the return of His children and, every time He sees one approaching, he runs to them!

Refuse to Return

The children of Israel began to believe life would be better if they simply returned to Egypt. Today, many Christians want to retreat from liberty in Christ and return to religion. Religion is thought to be easy because it provides a step-wise approach to redemption. However, even though relationship with the Father through Jesus may seem like work to the untrained eye, it is far simpler than any religion. After all, Jesus, Himself, said His yoke is easy and His burden is light!

> *Now, however, that you have come to be acquainted with and understand and know [the true] God, or rather to be understood and known by God, how can you turn back again to the weak and beggarly and worthless elementary things [of all religions before Christ came], whose slaves you once more want to become? (Galatians 4:9 AMP)*

There is no turning back! You don't want to go anywhere God's will isn't there!

> *Now the Lord is the Spirit, and where the Spirit of the Lord is, there is liberty (emancipation from bondage, freedom). (2 Corinthians 3:17)*

Jesus came to elevate us from servants to sons; from servility to empowerment. It's time for the Body of Christ to rise up and walk in the authority reserved for sons! And sons serve out of love – because they choose to – not out of obligation!

Sons are empowered. That empowerment is frequently referred to as "The Anointing."

"THE ANOINTING" AND SPIRITUAL GIFTS

O ne of the most frequently abused terms in the church is "the anointing." Listen long enough in church circles and you'll hear things like:

"My anointing to preach…"

"So and so is…anointed in song…"

"Such and such church is anointed…"

This is one of these things that sound religious…but it's dead wrong.

Before we get to the truth of what the anointing is, we need to establish what it is not. Contrary to popular belief, there is no double-portion, á lá Elisha (2 Kings 2:9), in the New Testament.

In other words, once you're born again, you get all the Jesus you're ever going to get. There are no "levels" in Christ – either you're in or you're not.

The Body of Christ, today, has a serious problem of laying claim to things in the Old Testament that have been superseded by the New Testament.

The truth of the matter is, every believer has the anointing of the Holy Spirit.

Let's take a look at Scripture and see what it has to say:

> *But if the Spirit of him that raised up Jesus from the dead dwell in you, he that raised up Christ from the dead shall also quicken your mortal bodies by his Spirit that dwelleth in you. (Romans 8:11)*

Did you catch that? The Holy Spirit dwells inside you! Therefore, the same anointing that Jesus had, you have access to that same power.

Which brings up a good question, what is the evidence of the anointing?

Glad you asked! There are two things that are key indicators of the anointing of God at work in your life.

The first is that the power at your disposal is ALWAYS used for the good of others. Check out the example of Jesus:

> *How God anointed Jesus of Nazareth with the Holy Ghost and with power: who went about doing good, and healing all that were oppressed of the devil; for God was with him. (Acts 10:38)*

Jesus always went about doing good. His example teaches us that the anointing and our gifting are not for our own use or benefit but for the benefit of others. In the aforementioned Scripture, it says that God anointed Jesus with the Holy Ghost. The Bible further tells us:

> *For in him we live, and move, and have our being; as certain also of your own poets have said, For we are also his offspring. (Acts 17:28)*

Through His Holy Spirit, we have been given new life.

Jesus also told us that we are to abide in him and His Word (His Spirit and Power) is to dwell in us (John 15:4-7).

The second evidence of the anointing of the Holy Spirit is far simpler and, yet, far more powerful.

Love.

Love is the dynamo of God's Kingdom. If faith is the currency of the Kingdom, love is what backs that currency. The Bible tells us that faith works by love (Galatians 5:6), which tells us that love is the power behind faith, without which, it is impossible to please God.

Love is so important that the Apostle Paul said that if we have all spiritual gifts and do not have love, we profit nothing; indeed, we are nothing (1 Corinthians 13:1-3)

Love is so important that Jesus, Himself, says this is the hallmark of discipleship:

> *By this shall all men know that ye are my disciples, if ye have love one to another. (John 13:35)*

Without the evidence of love, no one will be able to discern whether we are His disciples or not. If you have the anointing of the Holy Spirit, you will express and manifest it in love.

One of the greatest misconceptions in the Body of Christ, today, is the belief that the Holy Spirit can be taken away from you. Once again, this premise is derived from an Old Testament Scripture:

> *Cast me not away from thy presence; and take not thy holy spirit from me. (Psalms 51:11)*

This was perfectly acceptable for Old Testament Saints because they only had the Holy Spirit to *rest* upon them. However, because of our more excellent covenant (Hebrews 8:6), we have the *indwelling* of the Holy Spirit. But here's what Jesus said about the Holy Spirit:

> *And I will pray the Father, and he shall give you another Comforter, that he may abide with you for ever; (John 14:16)*

Did you catch that? Forever (for ever)! That's how long the Holy Spirit will be with us!

Now that we've established that the anointing is with every believer – eternally – and that it is the same for every believer, we need to discuss that which is different.

And that difference is gifting.

There is a difference between spiritual gifts and the gift of the Spirit. As I already mentioned, the gift of God is the Holy Spirit – He is the anointing. But there are also gifts from God.

If ye then, being evil, know how to give good gifts unto your children, how much more shall your Father which is in heaven give good things to them that ask him? (Matthew 7:11)

Some would say the most obvious answers are tongues and prophecy, but there's more than that.

And God hath set some in the church, first apostles, secondarily prophets, thirdly teachers, after that miracles, then gifts of healings, helps, governments, diversities of tongues. (1 Corinthians 12:28)

Now there are diversities of gifts, but the same Spirit. And there are differences of administrations, but the same Lord. And there are diversities of operations, but it is the same God which worketh all in all. But the manifestation of the Spirit is given to every man to profit withal. For to one is given by the Spirit the word of wisdom; to another the word of knowledge by the same Spirit; To another faith by the same Spirit; to another the gifts of healing by the same Spirit; To another the working of miracles; to another prophecy; to another discerning of spirits; to another divers kinds of tongues; to another the interpretation of tongues: But all these worketh that one and the selfsame Spirit, dividing to every man severally as he will. (1 Corinthians 12:4-11)

It is clear from the second passage of scripture, above, that it is the gifts from God that are diverse. However it is said these gifts will someday pass away (1 Corinthians 13:8). The good news is that they won't go away until the time when Jesus comes to reign eternally on earth.

Depending upon whom you ask, others may say ministry gifts are the the most obvious. Ephesians 4:11 illustrates the ministry gifts

> *And he gave some, apostles; and some, prophets; and some, evangelists; and some, pastors and teachers;*

And even these gifts have an expiration date – that is, when the saints are perfected (equipped – Ephesians 4:12), when we all come together in the unity of the faith and reach maturity in the stature of Christ (Ephesians 4:13), and when we are so rooted and grounded in faith that we aren't tossed around as children.

The point I'm making here is that the anointing is common to all believers but gifts are varied.

The one thing that both the gifts from God and the Gift of God have in common is that, once you have them, neither one is going anywhere. Romans 11:29 says it best:

> *For the gifts and calling of God are without repentance.*

That's good news!

Once we understand what we've been empowered with, we need to know how to flow it into the world.

THE FLOW OF THE GIFT

W e can know if a Church is truly the work of the Lord because of the manifestation of the fruit of the Spirit: Love, Joy, Peace, Longsuffering, Gentleness, Goodness, Faith, Meekness, and Temperance (Galatians 5:22-23). Additionally, the operation and recognition of ministry gifts (Ephesians 4:11-12) should be evident. If these things are not readily apparent, it may be the work of man or, worse, the work of the devil.

The purpose of the Church is to bring the will of God to the world. The purpose of the Pastor is to bring the Word of God to the people. And neither the Church nor the

Pastor is an advocate for religion but an ambassador of Kingdom relationship.

Religion defers reward; relationship decrees victory. Religion makes power abstract; relationship makes power available. Religion says you'll have it in the sweet-by-and-by; relationship says – because you're a child of the King – you already have it!

This understanding of what you have is not automatic. There's a process to it. There is a specific flow. You already have access to it…But you have to understand the flow in order appropriate it!

The process starts with the Head…

> *But the natural man receiveth not the things of the Spirit of God: for they are foolishness unto him: neither can he know them, because they are spiritually discerned. 15 But he that is spiritual judgeth all things, yet he himself is judged of no man. 16 For who hath known the mind of the Lord, that he may instruct him? But we have the mind of Christ. (Ephesians 2:14-16)*

The purpose of the pastor, as I mentioned earlier is to get the Word of God to people AND to be the frontline of discipleship. The first step in discipleship is to Get the Word of God into the heads of people to lead them to salvation and to get the same Word into the heads of the saints that they may grow into Kingdom maturity. The problem encountered by many in the Church is that we become impressed and led by "head knowledge." This is called "being carnal;" that is, driven by the flesh. Jesus told us to repent (change our mind) for the Kingdom of heaven is at hand. Through the Holy Spirit, prayer, study, and fellowship, you learn how to access the Kingdom and the wealth of its wisdom and benefits. But you can't stop there...

It has to enter the Heart...

> *8 But what saith it? The word is nigh thee, even in thy mouth, and in thy heart: that is, the word of faith, which we preach; 9 That if thou shalt confess with thy mouth the Lord Jesus, and shalt believe in thine heart that God hath raised him from the dead, thou shalt be saved. 10 For with the heart man believeth unto righteousness; and with the mouth confession is made unto salvation. (Romans 10:8-10)*

Once you hear the Word of God and it enters your head by your hearing, it then moves to your heart. There is an interesting thing that happens to you here – as you hear the Word through your outer ear, it is processed by your mind into your memory. As you recall what you've heard and speak the Word of God to yourself and your circumstances, you hear it in your inner ear. As you become faithful to repeat this process, the Word becomes fully digested in your spirit and, thus, enters your heart.

Your pastor (or any expounder of the Word of God) speaks the Word of God into your head but you speak it into your heart!

The Word, hidden in your heart, chastens you and keeps you righteousness-conscious. Having the Word preached in your hearing is key to your transformation by the renewing of your mind, which changes the way you think, which changes your state of being.

Don't believe me? Check this:

> *For as he thinketh in his heart, so is he: Eat and drink, saith he to thee; but his heart is not with thee. (Proverbs 23:7)*

So now we have the Word at hand in our head and in our heart. Now it's time to...

Express it in your House...

> *And Elisha said unto her, What shall I do for thee? tell me, what hast thou in the house? And she said, Thine handmaid hath not any thing in the house, save a pot of oil. (2 Kings 4:2)*

Joshua said something that should resonate with every believer who is the high priest of his household: "As for me and my house, we will serve the Lord!" (Joshua 24:15)

Once you move the Word of God from your head, to your heart, to your house, you not only invite God to change your paradigm, you are sowing seed for a paradigm shift for your family.

Here's a challenge to you: stop looking elsewhere for what you need. God has placed all you need at your disposal. The Word of God tells us that you have all sufficiency to abound to every good work? Take stock of your skill. Take stock of your supply. Take stock of your spirit. As a saint of God, you have all you need to abound to every good work. Can you abound if you're oppressed? Can you abound if you're sick? Can you abound if you're broke? No, no, and no!

If you take the time to read the story of the Widow's oil (2 Kings 4:1-7), you learn that God multiplied what she had in her house to the point it not only paid off her debt, but increased her with indefinite, ongoing substance. It is God's will to use what is close to us to sustain our posterity and ourselves!

The gift (Apostle, Prophet, Evangelist, Pastor, Teacher) shows the saints how to use the Word to call forth the substance of the storeroom of heaven into the shop floor of the earth realm. And when the saints understand how to access what they have in their house, operating out of love, the saints then learn how to pour into God's house!

We're working through our process roadmap and getting close to our destination.

We've taken the Word into our head, processed it into our heart, and moved it into our house. Now it must...

Flow to the Hand...

> And the Lord said unto him, What is that in thine hand? And he said, A rod. (Exodus 4:2)

The rod of Moses is an external representation of the power of God. Through the rod, Moses was able to effect signs and wonders that were intended to move Pharaoh to liberate the Israelites. However, the signs and wonders served to harden Pharaoh's heart and seek to retain them as slaves. New Testament saints, on the other hand, have the power of God within us – it is the same power that raised Jesus from the dead.

We have something the Old Testament saints didn't – The Spirit of the Lord (The Holy Spirit) inside us, whereas they only had it upon them!

When the Word of God is expressed in action – because faith without works is dead – we put our hand squarely on the plow without looking back!

When you get the Word into your head – because faith comes by hearing and hearing by the Word of God – you establish a changed mind and a repentant life...

But that's not enough...

When you get the Word into your heart – because out of the heart, flow the issues of life – you live a life of conviction and you die to sin and are awakened to righteousness...There is therefore, now, NO CONDEMNATION...

And that ain't enough...

When you move the Word into your house, you sow the seed – Jesus said THE WORD is THE SEED – that reproduces the change that God wrought in you into your family and your community...

And that still ain't enough...

When you manifest the Word into your hand, you put your faith into action. And if you're faithful to express in the earth with your hand, that which God has placed in your head and your heart and in your house, He will be faithful to prosper that what you set your hand to!

Flowing out what's been imparted to us depends upon our understanding of our power source.

PLUGGED IN, TURNED ON, TUNED IN

In order to manifest the Kingdom of God in the earth, we need to first access the power of God. To better understand this, I will use the analogy of a radio to express this concept. We need to be Plugged In, Turned On, and Tuned In so that we may accurately receive instruction and properly distribute the power of God in such a way that He is glorified and His children are helped.

And what is the exceeding greatness of his power to us-ward who believe, according to

270

the working of his mighty power, Which he wrought in Christ, when he raised him from the dead, and set him at his own right hand in the heavenly places, Far above all principality, and power, and might, and dominion, and every name that is named, not only in this world, but also in that which is to come. (Ephesians 1:19-21)

Plugged In

The first thing we need to understand is that God is the source of everything. And because Jesus is the express image of the Father, he represents the interface to the Father. Let me give you an illustration: power is only useable when you have the right interface. When electrical power is generated, it is done at between 200,000 and 400,000 volts. It is then transmitted via high-tension lines to substations that reduce the power to the 240 volts commonly used in the typical home. The device used to step this power to a useable level is called a transformer. Jesus is our transformer – the interface to the power of God. Without Him, attempting to access the power of God would prove futile at best and fatal at worst!

The first step in plugging into God is being Born Again. You have to be a natural-born Citizen of the Kingdom of God…because there are no illegal aliens in the Kingdom! Hence, in order to have hope of experiencing the power of God, we must be submitted to the power of God!

We have to be transformed by the renewing of our minds (Romans 12:2). We renew our minds by the Word of God. Immersion and study of – and meditating on and manifesting the Word of God are key to the constant process of renewing our minds. Jesus is the Word made flesh...do you get what I'm saying? It's Jesus who brings the power of God to our level.

All power belongs to God but God has delegated it to man (Genesis 1:26-28). Indeed, the very universe is suspended by the Word of God's Power (Hebrews 1:3). This was His original plan but sin interrupted that. However, glory to God, this is what Jesus came to restore!

Turned On

If you've contracted to have electrical power run to your house, it is available whenever you need it. When you need power to an appliance, you don't go back to the electric company and ask for power, you merely flip the switch.

Paul wrote in Ephesians 3:20...

> *Now unto him that is able to do exceeding abundantly above all that we ask or think, according to the power that worketh in us,*

Did you catch that – the power is within us! But, just in case you missed it...

> *But if the Spirit of him that raised up Jesus from the dead dwell in you, he that raised up Christ from the dead shall also quicken your mortal bodies by his Spirit that dwelleth in you. (Romans 8:11)*

The same power that raised Jesus from the dead dwells within you!

Jesus told his disciples to wait in Jerusalem until they received power (Acts 1:8). What was the power He spoke of? The power of the Holy Spirit! It is the Holy Spirit who convicts the unsaved of sin. It is the Holy Spirit who teaches us all things.

So, how do we flip the switch? By prayer, study, and fasting. Turning on the power of God means speaking God's Word to impossible situations. It's Mark 11 faith – speaking to mountains and being fully persuaded that they will move at your command! But understand, if you aren't connected to the power source, you cannot expect to benefit from the power. This is the difference between religion and relationship – religion makes power abstract; relationship makes power available!

Tuned In

WGOD – or KGOD for those of us west of the Mississippi – broadcasts 24x7x365. God's signal – the Holy Spirit – is always being broadcast. The Holy Spirit is everywhere at all times and His Program – sozo in Jesus – never changes. That sozo, the Greek word commonly associated with salvation from sin but it means so much more – deliverance from demonic oppression, bodily healing, AND material blessing.

The good news is that this broadcast always conveys Good News, and that there is good news for you. The bad news is that the revelation of this good news only comes when you are listening.

Right now, there are radio and television signals in this room. And you could, wrongly, conclude that because you don't perceive them with your natural senses that they are not there. However, turning on a radio or television and tuning in to a particular station, or making a call on a cell phone is evidence of the reality of these signals. Many folks, saved folks included, conclude that God's power is not available because they cannot perceive it with their senses. Sadly, this is one of the key reasons the church operates without power, today.

So, how do we tune in? This is the part of discipleship where disciples graduate from milk to meat. This is where we transition from knowing that God is able to knowing that God has already done it! This is where we transition from mere belief to faith.

Tuning in to Jesus means tuning out the world. When you're serious about tuning in to what God is saying, you realize the importance of tuning out those things that are not revealing what God is saying. This means turning off the TV, radio, worldly music, and online pursuits. Tuning in to God means getting alone with Him, like Jesus did:

> *And after he had dismissed the crowds, he went up on the mountain by himself to pray. When evening came, he was there alone,* (Matthew 14:23)

Tuning in to WGOD means exercising and manifesting your faith in a different way. Instead of *stressing*, it's *resting* in the certainty that God will do what He says in His Word. Tuning in means devoting some of your prayer time to silence – where you take as much time to listen as you do to talk.

Any musician knows that the rests in music are just as important as the notes. Well-placed silence adds depth and character to a musical piece. Silence in your prayer time avails you of the opportunity to hear what God is saying to you.

RELIGION, ITSELF

F ar be it from me to say I have all the answers…because I do not. However, there are a growing number of Bible scholars and teachers who are mounting very successful challenges to the traditional status quo and I am blessed to be among that number.

Throughout this book, I have taken aim at the fruit – here and now, though, I'm going after the root…

Religion.

In order to truly "Deconstruct Religion" we must first baseline a premise with a working definition. I found the following from the online etymology dictionary (http://www.etymonline.com):

> **religion (n.)**
> c.1200, "state of life bound by monastic vows," also "conduct indicating a belief in a divine power," from Anglo-French religiun (11c.), Old French religion "piety, devotion; religious community," and directly from Latin religionem (nominative religio) "respect for what is sacred, reverence for the gods; conscientiousness, sense of right, moral obligation; fear of the gods; divine service, religious observance; a religion, a faith, a mode of worship, cult; sanctity, holiness," in Late Latin "monastic life" (5c.).
>
> According to Cicero, it is derived from relegere "go through again" (in reading or in thought), from re– "again" (see re-) + legere "read" (see lecture (n.)). However, popular etymology among the later ancients (Servius, Lactantius, Augustine) and the interpretation of many modern writers connects it with religare "to bind fast" (see rely), via notion of "place an obligation on," or "bond between humans and gods." In that case, the re– would be intensive. Another possible origin is religiens "careful," opposite of negligens. In English, meaning "particular system of

faith" is recorded from c.1300; sense of "recognition of and allegiance in manner of life (perceived as justly due) to a higher, unseen power or powers" is from 1530s.

Wikipedia adds the following:

There is no precise equivalent of "religion" in Hebrew, and Judaism does not distinguish clearly between religious, national, racial, or ethnic identities. One of its central concepts is "halakha", sometimes translated as "law"", which guides religious practice and belief and many aspects of daily life.

That said, I postulate the following thesis:

Genesis 1 and 2 can be construed as God's "Mission Statement," that is, His original intent for creation can be gleaned from these two chapters. I have gone through these chapters from every angle I can conceive and have concluded the following: there is neither establishment nor endorsement of religion in the creation account, as there is a complete absence of any religious trappings (e.g., altars, temples, rituals, sacrifices). I have applied the same scrutiny to the Gospels as the account of redemption and have similarly found neither establishment nor endorsement of religion here, either. By these two premises, I conclude that it was neither God's plan in creation nor in redemption to establish any religion. God's plan in creation was to establish fellowship with His children. And, as this fellowship was broken by sin, it was restored in redemption. Like the definition listed above, the net result of religion is to bind, whereas life in Christ liberates (Luke 4:18-19, 2 Corinthians 3:17).

You have to take a leap of faith (pun intended) to build a case for religion in Scripture. Yes, it's there – but in every case, it emerges as a means by which men strive to relate to God outside the framework of relationship with Him, or a means by which man replaces Him. And when something manifests that scholars use to justify religion, it is something stemming from man missing God's intent and God having to implement something to cover man's erroneous attempts to reach Him.

First case in point: The first evidence of religion in Scripture occurs in Genesis 11 with the construction of the Tower of Babel. This was man's first attempt at building an edifice aimed at reaching God.

The second case in point, Exodus 19:10-25: In this account, God tells Moses to tell the people to sanctify themselves – abstain from food and drink; abstain from sex; wash yourselves and your clothing. They did as Moses instructed but out of fear and not of love. God wanted to speak to the people directly, as He did with Adam. However, the hearts of the people waxed fearful and when God spoke, the people cowered. When God saw their hearts, He gave them the Decalogue (10 Commandments – the prelude to the whole law). Do you see this? God didn't want to give His people the law; He wanted to give them Himself! Moreover, God wanted His children to be Kings and Priests, not to have an intermediary between them and Himself. But because of their fear, God established a priesthood that would endure to the advent of Jesus.

God had something to say about religion in Isaiah 1:10-17 – I like it best in The Message:

> *10 "Listen to my Message,*
> *you Sodom-schooled leaders.*
> *Receive God's revelation,*
> *you Gomorrah-schooled people.*
> *11-12 "Why this frenzy of sacrifices?"*
> *God's asking.*
> *"Don't you think I've had my fill of burnt sacrifices,*
> *rams and plump grain-fed calves?*
> *Don't you think I've had my fill*
> *of blood from bulls, lambs, and goats?*
> *When you come before me,*
> *whoever gave you the idea of acting like this,*
> *Running here and there, doing this and that—*
> *all this sheer commotion in the place provided for worship?*
> *13-17 "Quit your worship charades.*
> *I can't stand your trivial religious games:*
> *Monthly conferences, weekly Sabbaths, special meetings—*
> *meetings, meetings, meetings—I can't stand one more!*
> *Meetings for this, meetings for that. I hate them!*
> *You've worn me out!*
> *I'm sick of your religion, religion, religion,*

while you go right on sinning.
When you put on your next prayer-performance,
I'll be looking the other way.
No matter how long or loud or often you pray,
I'll not be listening.
And do you know why? Because you've been tearing
people to pieces, and your hands are bloody.
Go home and wash up.
Clean up your act.
Sweep your lives clean of your evildoings
so I don't have to look at them any longer.
Say no to wrong.
Learn to do good.
Work for justice.
Help the down-and-out.
Stand up for the homeless.
Go to bat for the defenseless.

If you catch this, you'll see that God doesn't hold religion in high esteem. Yet there is one area that must be addressed: James 1:27.

I call this one the refuge for the religious…

Pure religion and undefiled before God and the Father is this, To visit the fatherless and widows in their affliction, and to keep himself unspotted from the world. (James 1:27)

To understand this, we have to understand two things: audience and context. The audience in question was Hebrew Christians whose frame of reference were nearly five hundred years of over-the-top religion. After the last captivity of the Jews, the religious leaders (Pharisees, Sadducees, and Essenes) thought that religious zeal would keep them out of captivity. The context was an attempt to bring Christianity into relief for these new, albeit religious, believers. Moreover, why does James so acutely narrow his focus? If we are to observe and follow religious tenets, why doesn't James broaden the scope of what religion is? Certainly, his list would be more exhaustive!

This is one of those shining examples of where a doctrine is built around what is clearly a situational text. This passage of scripture was written to a specific audience with a specific context; it was not meant to apply to all readers.

So, what is the alternative to religion? That would be a relationship with our Heavenly Father through Jesus. This relationship is possible by God's Grace (His Part) through Faith (our part).

In the beginning, there was the Godhead and His creation. In fact, when God created the environment for man, He spoke to substance and called things to be. However, when God created man, He spoke to Himself, drawing His crowning creation out of Himself! God and man had unbridled, unfettered fellowship. God spoke to Adam and Adam talked with God. Everything man needed or wanted was at his disposal. Then sin entered in and caused this fellowship to be broken.

Enter Jesus.

Jesus is the lamb slain from the foundation of time. He is not God's "plan B;" he is the eternal answer for every question and every problem. When Jesus showed up, mankind received redemption and reconciliation. And that reconciliation and redemption is made manifest to all who repent (change their minds) from sin. In fact, Jesus made an extraordinary statement in Luke 19:10:

> For the Son of Man is come to seek and to save **that** which was lost (emphasis mine).

Notice He used an impersonal pronoun, not a personal. He did not say they, them, who, or whom! I can say with certainty, that religion IS NOT what He came to seek or to save; rather it was the dominion authority given to man in Genesis 1:26-28! Once the Kingdom was fully manifest on earth, Jesus could complete his redemptive work.

My gauntlet is this, as I throw it to the ground, there is no Biblical support for religion. I will close with the words of our Lord and Savior, Jesus Christ:

> [19] Go then and make disciples of all the nations, baptizing them into the name of the Father and of the Son and of the Holy Spirit, [20] Teaching them to observe everything that I have commanded you, and behold, I am with

you all the days (perpetually, uniformly, and on every occasion), to the [very] close and consummation of the age. Amen (so let it be). (Matthew 28:19-20 AMP)

Jesus never said, "Go and establish a religion in my name." Why, then, have folks insisted on doing something they were never instructed to while ignoring "Heal the sick…" and "Raise the dead…" things they are instructed to do?

Let's get out and get busy doing the things Jesus told us to do instead of busying ourselves with things He never commanded!

ABOUT THE AUTHOR

Derrick Day is the founder and Pastor of Agape Dominion Outreach (www.agapedominion.org) in Surprise, Arizona and Founding Bishop of Kingdom Covenant, a ministry governance and church planting organization. He is the husband of Angela and the father of five sons. Derrick has been faithfully studying, preaching, and teaching the uncompromised Word of God for nearly thirteen years. In addition to his labor in the Kingdom of God, he is a consultant in software engineering, a former columnist with the Norfolk, Virginia New Journal and Guide, and a former radio talk-show host at WNIS News Radio in Norfolk, Virginia. Derrick also served in the

United States Navy, honorably discharged after seven years. He is a native of Detroit, MI.

Derrick is an avid blogger and dynamic public speaker. He is available to preach, teach, or speak at your next event. You can contact him at www.derrickday.com.

Made in the USA
Middletown, DE
11 January 2019